WA

SO-BDC-345

LOVERS IN MARRIAGE

LOVERS IN MARRIAGE

Louis Evely

Translated by John Drury

HERDER AND HERDER

1968
HERDER AND HERDER NEW YORK
232 Madison Avenue, New York, N.Y. 10016

Original edition: *Amour et mariage,*
published by the author.

Nihil obstat: Thomas J. Beary, Censor Librorum
Imprimatur: ✠ Robert F. Joyce, Bishop of Burlington
May 17, 1968

Library of Congress Catalog Card Number: 68–29886
© 1968 by Herder and Herder, Inc.
Manufactured in the United States

CONTENTS

LOVERS IN MARRIAGE

CHAPTER 1

Fidelity

Let me put forward a rather unsettling question about marriage. Does marriage fan the fires of love or extinguish them?

Statistically speaking, the answer is all too clear. Just ask our young people how many homes they have found to serve as patterns for their future household. However, my question is not just about things as they are; it is about things as they should be. Does this "institution," marriage, nourish and stimulate and deepen love? Or does it stifle love and eventually do away with it altogether?

Every authentic love begets a bond of fidelity, an institution. But what are we to say of institutions where there is no love? We will have to take a closer look at this thing called fidelity.

What is it that you promise when you get married? To stick together even if you no longer love each other? To love each other forever? Are you pledging fidelity to a person or to an institution?

Can you really promise someone that you will love him forever? What could such a commitment possibly mean? Is it an act of sheer will power, a dedicated effort, or a presumptuous boast? Who can say what he or she will be or will feel thirty years from now?

Let us not reduce fidelity to a purely negative quantity: "I'll never leave you." Or worse still: "I'll never be unfaithful to you." "Father, I'm faithful to my wife. I've never played around." Is that it? Is that what you promised her?

The Sunday Mass obligation offers an interesting analogy. You say, "I go to Mass every Sunday. I wouldn't miss Sunday Mass for anything in the world." Do you think that satisfies God? Do you think the Lord is content if you do not miss Mass? Or does he want you to make it an offering of praise, of thanks, and of brotherhood, to go because you need and want to go? And do you think your spouse is content with a lesser type of fidelity?

What, then, does fidelity mean? What does it involve? You will see that I closely associate fidelity to God and fidelity to a person. As I see it, God is a person; so it comes down to the same thing.

Faith itself is fidelity; that is why we can talk about "marital faith." That is what a person gives in marriage. And the best definition of faith that I can think of is this: faith is something which keeps our eyes fixed on God. This is a beautiful definition because it tells us right away that faith is something we never possess definitively.

Faith is not the recitation of the creed, the profession of certain dogmas, or the performance of certain rites. Faith is a living relationship with some person, from whom I expect a great deal, whom I never cease to know better, to think about, to discover. Well, conjugal faith is exactly the same. Once you think you "have" faith, you no longer do. The person who says "I have faith" or "I have the truth" is a pharisee, treating God as though he were a personal possession.

What is truth for you: a person or a thing? For us, it is a

person: "I am the Truth." So you never *have* the truth; you have, rather, a living relationship with it. You say, "I have a wife," or "I have a husband." And right at that moment you no longer do, you poor soul. When you reach the point where you think you possess a person, you have lost him. You can possess a *thing*. You can familiarize yourself with all its parts and get to know it inside out. But a person—that is a different story!

Do you want to know the best definition of "person"? A person is a being who has a future that far exceeds his past and his present. A person has an unlimited future. He has nothing less than eternity itself in which to develop all his potentialities and to reveal all the possibilities that exist in him.

This being so, what are we to say when we see people who are dried-up fossils at twenty-five, thirty, thirty-five? There must be something terribly wrong with life and with marriage. These people are supposed to go on developing for all eternity, and they have come to a halt already. Only a small number of people are truly alive.

The first religious, moral, and conjugal obligation is this: to be alive. But no one questions himself on this obligation.

Are you still alive?

Do you still have a living relationship with each other?

Do you still have a future to share?

A person is a being whose future is much more than his past and his present. In other words, his best is yet to come. If you do not believe that, do not bother getting married, for you are going to be terribly bored.

A person's best will only come out if it is discovered and brought out, and that calls for a lot of effort. You still do not really know each other. If tomorrow your husband were loved by

11

a real woman, if tomorrow your wife were loved by a real man, what discoveries and happy transformations would take place! But, alas, you are already married.

There is a wonderful story in the Bible, a passage from an apocryphal text. Sarah and Abraham set out for Egypt because there is a famine. They have been married for a good number of years. While they are journeying, some Egyptian men eye Sarah and tell Abraham, "Your wife is very beautiful." And the Bible remarks simply that Abraham looked at Sarah and saw that she was indeed beautiful. It had been a long time since he really looked at her.

Now and then a person may say to you, "You're lucky enough to be a Christian. It must be wonderful to have faith." You are stunned. All of a sudden you realize that it has been a long time since you really thought about your faith.

Now this is what I am trying to say: nothing can be lost so easily and so readily as love and faith. As you see, for me conjugal faith and conjugal love are synonymous. Love is the faith that you have in each other. Faith and hope and love go together. Our spouse always embodies much more than we have already discovered in him or her.

To love someone is to give that person credit for having more than we have found in him. What do you expect of each other? Do you give each other credit for having more than is already evident? Does the routine part of your marriage, the part you take for granted, outweigh the thrill of surprise and discovery? That is the critical question about your marriage.

Gabriel Marcel gives a very beautiful definition of love: to love someone is to have unending hope in him. Love necessarily has a future dimension. When you were engaged to be married, the two of you made countless plans for the future. Do you still do this? If, at 50, you are not making plans for your future life together, then you no longer love each other.

Love means putting your trust in someone and giving him credit. When a wife feels she knows her husband, when she has him boxed and classified, she no longer loves him. When a husband thinks he knows his wife, when he is no longer attentive, when he no longer speaks or listens to her, then he no longer loves her. In thinking that he knows her, he shows that he no longer knows her. She is turned into a thing, and ceases to be a person for him. This is usually the moment when someone else begins to notice her, and she becomes so happy that one can hardly recognize her.

When you think you know someone, you no longer love him. When a parent passes final judgment on his child, when he claims to know what his child is "really like," when he fails to leave room for the infinite potential within his child, then he does not love his child any longer.

The havoc which this presumed knowledge can cause is frightening. Many children are better persons outside the home because there people still believe in them; at home, their parents claim to know them. Without trust there can be no growth. We can grow only so long as someone believes in us, so long as someone loves us.

When children reach the age of fifteen or sixteen, their parents often stop loving them; to be precise, they think they know them. So the child turns to someone else: a teacher, a friend, a sweetheart—someone who believes in them and will allow them to grow. We grow only for people who believe in us, who trust us and love us. Is your spouse still growing? Do you still give your spouse credit for more than you know? What do you expect of your spouse? Do you still respect the dimension of mystery which surrounds this person?

The story of Zachary, the father of John the Baptist, has a lesson for us. He was a high priest, advanced in years. He was a man of faith, and he had preserved a fidelity of sorts; but it was a negative fidelity, the kind we are wont to substitute for a real, living fidelity.

Zachary still performed the duties of his ministry. He prayed, he performed the liturgical service when it was his turn; but his heart had turned cold and he no longer expected anything of God. He had been asking for a child for a long time, but he had never gotten one. He continued to pray, but he no longer believed. He had remained faithful to his promise all right, but he had not remained faithful to his love. That is the worst danger facing a marriage: to remain faithful to the promise you have made, thinking that you are thereby excused from being faithful to your love.

Which is better: love without marriage, or marriage without love? Which would you choose? Do you think your marriage has helped your love? Would you devote more effort to your love if you were not married?

The whole New Testament almost runs aground on the hardheartedness and withered fidelity of an old priest. When he is told that he will get the son he has longed for, he does not believe it: "It's not possible. It's too late, at my age. (Everyone uses that line!) Look at my wife, for God's sake; she's sterile. What can one hope to get from her?" Now do you begin to see what fidelity demands of us? Do you begin to see what hope love exacts from us? To hope at eighty that your wife will give you new life: that is how much love demands of us.

Nothing creeps over us so unawares as death, whether it be

death to God or death to human beings. I want to stress this point because it is so common. If you stop writing, you soon lose the desire to write. If you stop talking, you soon have nothing to say. To be sure, married people often find that they can communicate with each other without saying a word. But if you stop looking at each other, you will soon find that you will not even see each other. And it all happens unawares, without any conscious intention.

The worst sin of all is the sin of omission. A home is not destroyed by quarrels, by unforeseen difficulties, by money crises, or even by infidelity. What destroys a home is the rut of routine. When, without realizing it, you stop looking at each other, or talking to each other, or quarreling with each other, then the household is in danger.

I want to stress this point because I have a lot of experience: not in marriage, but in the religious life. It is exactly the same. For a few months you really relish the taste of prayer; then suddenly, the savor is gone and prayer becomes a matter of indifference to you.

Nothing is easier to learn than prayer. Go on retreat for a few days and you soon acquire a facility for prayer. The first time around, 10 minutes of meditation seem like an hour. But soon you are doing 45 minutes without batting an eye. It is so easy to learn—and it can be forgotten just as quickly. Love, alas, is no different; in fact, it is exactly the same.

Nothing is easier than to stop living. And I am really afraid that marriage, as an institution, is an invitation to stop being aware, to stop living.

Married people feel that they have something, that they are set up in something solid. They are, after all, united in a marriage and it is indissoluble.

The indissolubility of marriage often seems to be a juridical guarantee. Ask someone what it means and they will say, "We cannot be separated." Notice the negative cast of that remark. Is that what indissolubility means to you, that you cannot be separated? Well, I say you would be better off separated, alive and loving someone else, than living together like two dead people. You would be better off separated, and loving someone, because the worst sin of all is to be dead and the easiest temptation is to let marriage, as an institution, become an opiate, a dead-letter file.

If that is all indissolubility means to you, then we are enmeshed in juridical forms and the Church is fostering hypocrisy. How can we go on with an institution that degrades people in this way? It is a question we must face.

Is your marriage degrading you? Or is it ennobling you?

Is it keeping you alive? Or is it killing you?

There is another line of escape which I would like to examine before I get on a more positive track. It goes something like this: "Ah, but we have to think of the children." As soon as you say that, you have lost: because it proves that you have nothing else; besides, it is completely negative and, what is more, it is not true.

The existence of children is not the justification for marriage; it definitely is not.

You may think I am a little odd. But I tell you that the children would be happier in a second marriage that succeeds than in a first marriage that has run aground. To fall back on the children is to prove the inanity of the conjugal bond. We must take them into account, of course, because we are responsible for them. But what the children need most is not that you love *them* but that you love *each other*.

16

Do you realize that if you stay together for their sake alone, you are cutting off their future and squelching their desire to grow up? What will they think? "It's nice to be a child because people love you. But adults aren't happy; they don't give or get love from anyone." Then and there they lose the desire to grow up.

Some day, it seems to me, children will have to be ruled out in the first few years of marriage. Nowadays boy-girl contacts are taking place earlier and earlier. There is greater freedom but maturity comes later. Education is a longer process, conviction grows slowly, but opportunity is close at hand.

Moreover, as I see it, most marriages are invalid. And that brings us to another important question. What is a valid marriage?

A sacrament presupposes a human act; it sanctifies some human value. Today we tend to bless and sanctify things at random. But can we really sanctify a passing fancy? Can we sanctify the legitimation of a child? Certainly not, because the necessary human act is not present. To commit a mortal sin, there must be full knowledge and full consent. Must we not demand the same things for a marriage?

We should bring a child into the world only after we have prepared a proper home for him. If one wants an infant, it is his interest that should be considered. Would he be happy to be born into this household? Is it stable and happy enough to give him a good home?

Right now the would-be parents consider their own desires: "Do *we* want an infant?" How about a dog instead?

Children are not the purpose of marriage, nor the cement for it. Stay together for the children's sake and you will kill them. If you must stay together for their sake, it can only be because you love each other, not because you are shackled to each other.

Well, then, what is the meaning of indissolubility? What is the meaning of conjugal fidelity? Let me try to answer these questions.

I think a person can be faithful only to himself. It is impossible for me to be faithful to someone else, to pretend that I shall love this other person forever. I think you can only make one promise to another person: "I shall keep myself alive, I shall not fade out into unconsciousness, I shall not forget that you are alive."

We can only be faithful to ourselves. We can promise only to be faithful in keeping ourselves alive. I did not promise you fidelity. Who knows what will happen in the future? Besides, it is not infidelity which wrecks marriages. But I did promise to love you, and to keep myself alive for your sake. If I have stopped loving you, it is only because I have stopped being alive.

I want to start being alive all over again, so that I can start loving you all over again. That and that alone is the fidelity I pledge you. I cannot promise to love you for a lifetime. But I can promise to stay alive; and if I do stay alive, and if there is real love at the roots of this whole thing, then I think that this love of ours will stay alive and that, if it should falter, we can bring it back to life. But notice what I said: a real love at the roots. It cannot be a pipe dream or a whim, even one sanctioned by a contract.

What does it mean to love someone? It means that we are ushered into his or her real life, that we know who he or she really is, that we live as we have never really lived before, that we become ourselves as we never were before, that two "I's" become a "we" and then more themselves than they ever were before. And the process renews itself and goes on unceasingly, despite problems and separations and conflicts.

When two people really love each other, they help each other to stay alive and to grow. They come to know each other as no one has ever known them before. Love is not a blindfold, it is an eye-opener. There is one kind of lucidity that is sad, of course: judging someone on the basis of his past. But there is another kind of clarity that only comes with love: imagining what a person is capable of becoming.

You begin to love each other when you begin to make something of each other. You stop loving each other when you try to make a sure thing of each other. You can begin to love each other again only when you begin again to make something of each other, when you start living again and changing together.

And when a person is loved like that, he must remain faithful to such a love. The being who has been revealed to him by this love must stay alive. If I am faithful only to another, then I run the risk of letting myself die at the same time. How many people are more alive outside their marriage than they are within it! But real fidelity is staying alive.

Now I have something uncomplimentary to say about men. Men do not carry off marriage very well. For a woman, marriage is a beginning; for most men, it is a finale. Our hero expends much effort in winning the lady, and then he takes his new possession home and forgets her. Most women are widows the day after their marriage. She marries a dashing courtier, she comes home to a man whose mind is somewhere else. The man's fiancée ends up as a trinket, and the interminable boredom begins.

A woman takes her home to heart; she puts her whole self into it. A man saves himself for his work, his amusements, his buddies. Most men are not truly adult because they are too much occupied with things. A woman is naturally oriented towards human beings. Outside the home, the men I know are charming, gay, and sociable; at home, however, they are ill at ease, bumps on a log. Men seem to be afraid of such personal commitments; they do not relish deep human relations. They work with a ready will, they enjoy social contacts and get-togethers. But only rarely does it happen that a man is truly alive with his family, that he is a friend and a conversationalist for his wife, that he is a real father to his children.

A woman is naturally a mother. Even if she does not have a child, she knows all about motherhood. For a man, however, fatherhood is a long apprenticeship. Marriage should be a fresh school of learning for him, where he learns to become a man, a spouse, a father. But marriage as an institution unfortunately seems to put him to sleep; he rests contentedly with his new-found pride of ownership.

Is it not the ideal that a man maintain his hold on his wife through her own free will? Would you want to hold her to an institution? And how can it be free if it is not a deliberate choice, maintained and renewed over and over again through an enduring love? What purpose does the institution serve?

So someone will say to me, "Ah, well, Father, you don't know anything about love or about marriage. If married people weren't tied together, they'd be parted ten times over." I readily admit that love has its lapses. I know there are times when a person feels he no longer loves someone he really does love. Every child thinks about running away from home.

Of course, the heart has its bad moments. But what makes up for these lapses and bad moments? What is the remedy for them: a law? an institution? No, because then you let the law excuse you from loving each other. The remedy for love's failings is love itself. Having experienced such lapses, love knows that it has not ceased to exist when it feels these lapses coming on. The experience of love, not some legal prescription, provides love's remedy.

The danger in your legal tie is that you will fall back on it when you feel that you no longer love each other, instead of nourishing and re-enkindling the love you no longer feel.

The most beautiful definition of fidelity is: to be faithful to what you have seen in the light when the times of darkness come. Faith is a kaleidoscope of light and shadow. The person who always has light is living in the world of visions, not in the world of faith. The person who is always in darkness cannot have faith. If you have faith, then you have had some moments of light. And you cannot deny what you saw in the light when the dark moments come. Why not? (This must be pointed out to some of our contemporaries who have the wrong idea about sincerity, who want to be sincere every single moment of their existence.) Because when you are in the dark you know that you do not see, just as you know you do see when you are in the light. In the dark you cannot deny what you knew in the light.

It is the same thing in marriage. You know that when you loved each other, life was transformed and you grew wondrously. Knowing that she had this power over you, and you over her, you have faith that this gift will return, because love does not die.

If marriage is indissoluble it is not because the law says so; it is because that is the nature of true love. But if there is no true love at the start, there is nothing there at all; there is not even a valid sacrament.

Do not tell me that the law, the institution, protects us from our own whims. What protects us is our love. We know how to re-enkindle our love—that is our protection. I put up with the bad spells because it is real love, not because I can fall back on an institution.

Do you hold your spouse of her own free will? If you were not married, would you no longer love each other? You must ask yourself this important question. Perhaps if you were not falling back on your "rights" you would become disquiet and attentive.

Genuine love is always a bit disquiet. It must be a little disquiet; in other words, it must be creative. Note well: I do not mean the disquiet of jealousy or doubt; I mean the disquiet of inventiveness. You cannot say the same thing to a person twice because, the second time around, it is less true; because the other person has changed in the meantime. You just cannot say the same thing twice, unless you put it a little differently, unless you are inventive.

Speaking is not a matter of saying something that is on your tongue; it involves the ear of another. Speaking is a relation between two people, who are continually changing. So if you repeat the same words, you actually say something different the second time. You must say it differently the second time, if you want to make the same point. Well then, imagine how inventive you must be in telling your wife that you love her! It is a fatiguing job for a man. Many husbands give up and take the easy way out: they remain "faithful."

To grow, a person must be loved. To love a person is to love a being capable of growing indefinitely. And the sad fact is that the bosom of the family is a burial ground for many. There they are "known," there they have no chance for growth or change, they find no response to the overtures they make. Each family member cannot see the feeble groping of the others, because he is too wrapped up in his own needs. He does not open up to the others, he does not even see them. Each sees what the others have failed to do, none sees what the others have managed to do. No one wants to risk the pain involved in each feeble attempt at creation.

Yet, as I see it, marriage is made up of these silent signals across the wastes of solitude. Each signal seems faint and fragile, but the solid stuff of marriage is woven of these signals. They express and carry on the breath of life.

When you became engaged, someone in the family probably said, "Ah, you seem to be transformed. Well, you're living in a dream world, you'll soon snap out of it." More than likely you have. More than likely you no longer dream together. More than likely you no longer create one another.

Love is a creative force. It becomes true and valid only insofar as it exerts creative power over the other party. Apart from love, there is no truth to this person. Your wife becomes a woman only insofar as you make her a woman. The value of marriage as an institution is the value of the love that it expresses, the value of the love which animates it. Without love, the institution is the letter of the law without the spirit of the law. Those who cling blindly to it will become fossils.

Herein lies the positive connotation of marital "indissolubility": *when love has existed,* when it has created two beings, it can always bring them to life once again and create them anew.

Christ would never have instituted such a law if it were a law of death, counseling fidelity in death. In reality, it is a law of life and resurrection. The revelation of Christ is the revelation of a love which nothing can discourage or wear down. It is a love which gives thanks even on the cross, because it is sure it will save and resurrect those who crucify it. It is a love capable of reviving love.

That transition may have seemed very abrupt, but the whole thing is tied together. Did Christ give us a law, or a promise of life? I really think you can hold a spouse only of her own free will, only by continually creating each other, only by growing together unceasingly. What holds you together is not a law, or a sacrament, or an obligation that binds under pain of mortal sin: the only thing that holds you together is a free act of consent that is continually renewed.

It is true that you are sometimes tempted to slip into forgetfulness, to stop being alive. It is the worst sin of all, and we commit it all the time. The more I look around, the more dead people I find walking around. Only a handful of people seem to keep on learning, thinking, and changing. But how can there be love without that?

Here then is the first thing for your examination of conscience. What an important first step it is to admit that we have stopped living: "I have stopped loving you only because I have stopped being alive. I stopped living when I stopped bringing you to life, when I stopped admiring you and expecting the unexpected from you, when I stopped letting you radiate life and joy." And, as far as I am concerned, the only fidelity one can promise is this: "I shall start living again in order to start loving you again."

Nothing is easier than dying, and this is true of every aspect of human life: prayer, religious practice, faith, friendship, family relations, conjugal life. Even beyond your love for each other, you have the right to demand that your partner keep on living. Herein lies the source of marital disputes, which are a summons to start living once again.

Two people are no longer united if they have become two inert *things*. Placed side by side, two inanimate objects get in each other's way. Only two *persons* can truly live together, communicating to each other and letting their real selves shine through. The vitality of one makes the other more real and alive, more truly himself. Instead of being a stumbling block to each other, two persons permit each other to open out and grow.

Your conjugal relationship must be measured by your commitment to stay truly alive. So now you can see why Christ said, "I have come that you may have life, and have it in more abundance." That is why he gave up his life. He said to himself, "These creatures are so *dead*." It was not that men were so wicked or sinful, it was that they were so dead.

Actually, for 30 years Christ set an example for men. Then he realized that no one was paying any attention to his example. Although he set an example in the ordinary round of everyday life, no one paid any attention. So for three years he preached and explained his message, just as many women try to talk to their husbands during the first years of their marriage. But even that did not work. So Christ said to himself, "I'll have to do something more drastic. My words, my miracles, my example were to no avail; I must give up my life for them. I must love them strongly enough to bring them back to life." And that is what he did: he gave men the gift of his own life in order to restore them to life.

The first duty of a married person is to stay alive, to maintain his love and interest in his spouse and his children, to help them grow into the persons that they are.

CHAPTER 2

The Purpose of Human Life

Love for one's spouse, like love for God, is a faith that can fade away and come back to life again. We look on God as someone who is ever new and inexhaustible. Well, substitute "love" for "God" and you can retain the same attributes. Love, too, is ever new and inexhaustible. It allows a person to realize his or her infinite potential.

Marriage, like faith, puts us in a living relationship with another; it keeps our gaze oriented to that other person. Marriage, like faith, is attacked by the same enemy: routine. Marriage, like faith, is nourished and kept alive by attentiveness and hopeful expectation.

To love is to dream, to picture the infinite potential that lies shrouded in the mysterious personality of another. The Gospel forbids us to judge others. We should get to know them, of course, but true knowledge of another reveals how much we do not yet know about them. The wise man knows he is ignorant of many things.

Do not act like a sophomore where love is concerned. Do not think that you know everything. If you are truly wise about love, you know that much about your loved one is hidden from you. If you are truly wise about love, you will not treat your loved one as an inert object.

Our knowledge, to a large extent, is restricted to surface features. We should not love a person for his or her odious traits; that is stupid. Neither should we stop trying to know a person so that we might go on loving them; that is ridiculous. Authentic love means total clarity, it means taking into account the hidden dimensions of another which have not yet come to light. It means addressing oneself to these dimensions so that they can be brought out into the light.

You do not know the best part of yourself. The best that is in you can well up gradually from moment to moment. Notice what Christ did. He treated people as if no one had ever known or loved them before. He treated people as if they were fledglings, still open to growth. He looked at the publicans and sinners, at Zachaeus, Mary Magdalene, and Matthew the publican, and he saw that they had stopped growing because people had stopped loving them.

At what point did you stop loving yourself? At what point did you stop growing, and relinquish your responsibility for the development of your spouse? At what point did you freeze over?

A person is a hidden depth of infinite expanse. Herein lies the field for ever new discoveries. But the temptation is to stay on the surface and explore only there.

Don Juan is the symbol of impotence in love. He is like the wandering Jew, looking outside himself for a freedom that he no longer possesses within. True freedom means exploring the hidden dimensions within and making ever new discoveries there. At the surface level there are not many discoveries to be made.

When the person by your side is no longer a sign of the infinite, when this person is a fixed entity in time and space, it is a terrible situation. For everything and everyone is a sign of something greater than himself. And marriage is a process of

27

carrying this sign to its ultimate destiny; in short, it is an endless process.

As I stressed earlier, marital fidelity is not like the fidelity of the iron wheel to the railroad track. Authentic fidelity is the result of an authentic love, and it can flare back to life time and again. You remember what love did for you at the start. It opened up a whole new world to you and you saw yourself in an entirely new light. Well, conjugal fidelity and the sacrament of marriage involve simply this: believing that you are capable of being resurrected over and over again—not simply on the last day but every day.

The real question is: Have you been resurrected? Has anyone ever loved you so much that you came back to life? Has anyone ever pardoned you in such a way that your joy surpassed that which you experienced when you were an innocent lamb? Do you believe that in the world there exists a being, a love, a summons that is capable of resurrecting you? Have you really experienced it?

I can believe in resurrection only if I have experienced it. That is why there can be a valid marriage only if there is an authentic love involved. Belief in resurrection presupposes the experience of resurrection.

Faith is too often emptied of any real content. "I believe everything that you have revealed." How empty that is! For to believe everything is to believe nothing. An old general was once asked what he believed. He replied, "If you want to know what I believe, you'll have to ask Rome." He believed in his faith!

Do you realize that you cannot believe in someone if you do not know him? You cannot and you should not! It is only when you know someone that you believe him. On the basis of what you know about him, you are willing to take his word for what you do not yet know.

Faith is primarily an experience. I believe in the resurrection because I myself have been resurrected. If you have not had such an experience, then your faith in the resurrection is an empty thing. It only means that you refuse not to believe.

As long as we are on this point, let me say something about the acts of faith, hope, and charity that we usually say in our prayers. They are really pretty silly. "O my God, I love you above all things . . ." How presumptuous and hypocritical! Love is a grace that we ask for. As a friend of mine once said, "I know only one formula for the act of charity: My God, I believe with all my heart that you love me with all your heart." Notice how much better that is!

So then, we cannot believe in the resurrection without having experienced the resurrection. And the only way you can believe that your love will come to life again is by the fact that it was alive once upon a time and brought you back to life. Otherwise the Christian law and the state law are dehumanizing things. To spend your life with someone you do not love would be a scandalous and degrading thing. Truly, there is much more prostitution in marriage than outside marriage.

Which is more sinful: to go to bed with someone you do not love in marriage, or to go to bed with someone you do love outside of marriage? It is a question you should ask yourself.

Heine once said: "Nothing is more degrading than a noble act performed in an ignoble spirit." An act of charity performed to draw attention to oneself, a heroic act done for show. We cannot live our marriage out of ignoble motives, resigning ourselves to ignoble efforts.

Marriage is living a life of love. Your children need the love you have for each other. There is growing unanimity among psychologists that nothing is more harmful to a child than a home where there is no love—whether the couple stays together or not. The separation is readily evident to the child, whether they live together or not.

I know it is dangerous to talk about these things, because people are easily shook up when you start questioning things. Transitions are always dangerous. Too many Christians have been excused from having a conscience because they have the commandments. Too many Christians have been excused from living a life because they have a law. And when one tries to bring them from one to the other, they come apart at the seams.

Let me get back to the Sunday Mass obligation once again. A person goes to Mass to avoid mortal sin. It is a scandalous attitude and a degrading one. Remember: nothing is more dangerous than a noble act performed in an ignoble spirit. Now picture a mother saying, "If you don't come to see me every Sunday, if you don't come to dinner—I don't care whether you eat or not—I'll kill you."

Most Christians picture the Church as that kind of mother. As they see it, it is the Church that cuts them off from God. She has invented a mortal sin of her own. They would like to remain in touch with God and the Church, but the Church cuts them off. It is a terrible way to look at it. One of my friends studied the proceedings of the ancient council which promulgated this law, and he found that the intent was quite different. The faithful must take spiritual nourishment regularly because they will soon forget about God if they do not go to see him regularly; they will soon have nothing to say to him if they do not speak to him regularly. And once a week seemed to be the required rate of intercontact.

Thus it is not the Church that cuts you off from God; it is you yourself. Weekly attendance is a reminder for your conscience, but most people take it for a law. People go on Sunday, to be sure, but they are dead going in and dead coming out. And when they have a good reason for not going on Sunday, do not think that they go on Monday. The law has gone by the boards!

Do you know what happens when you try to explain all this to people? They go away saying, "We don't have to go to Mass on Sunday any more. It's not obligatory. We were brainwashed." So they stop going to Mass on Sunday. They decide that they will look for God in the country or on the beach. Going to Mass becomes a thing of the past. Nothing, you see, is more risky than trying to wean people from laws to self-motivated activity.

So you think that marriage is an obligation to fidelity, and that this obligation excuses you from loving each other. You show up, you play the game; but you do not love. You are married, you have a law to hold on to; so you do not keep on living. It is a terrible situation, but it is the real plight of many.

Marriage is a commitment to love. As I pointed out earlier, fidelity to this commitment means that you promise to keep yourself alive. And how difficult it is to keep that promise! How difficult it is to refrain from passing final judgment on your spouse, to avoid treating your spouse as a personal possession, to keep on expecting great things from him or her. When Jesus explained the meaning of love to his disciples, they remarked cynically, "If that is the way it is, then it is better not to have a

31

wife at all." That seems to be the spontaneous reaction of most people.

Now I should like to tackle another question: What is the purpose of man's life? What are we supposed to be doing here?

Up until the twentieth century, work seemed to be the purpose and the end of human life. Men lived to work and people got married to procreate children. Men had their jobs and women had the pangs of "labor." There was a certain consistency.

Now, for the first time in modern history, we are facing a civilization where leisure is an important item. What this means is that a man can choose a line of work that will enhance his self-development, that he does not have to choose a job which he does not like. And note well that "choosing a line of work" is not the same as "not having to work"; to keep a man from working would be the worst punishment of all.

At the same time there is a changed outlook in the Church itself. Since Vatican II we have begun to see the relationship and development of the spouses as the fundamental purpose of marriage. Procreation is included within this purpose, of course, since marital love strives to create something; but it is the fruit of marriage, not its purpose. To get married in order to have children could mean that you really do not love each other. Children are the fruit of marital love, not the purpose of marriage.

The purpose of human life is to learn how to love. In this world nothing is more sacred than our relationship with others. The Gospel and, more importantly, our own experiences tell us that. Clearly, the most precious moments in our life are those in which we have shared a close communion with someone else.

The noblest and most beautiful mission in life is to spread the conviction that we have only one purpose here: to love and be loved our whole life long. Can you think of any other purpose for us? The husband lies down in the rut of his own routine, the wife entombs herself in the atmosphere of the home. They work, they carry on; but it is a living death. Better to bury them now.

Has there ever been a time in the past when men really saw what the purpose of human life was? What other purpose could there be except to learn how to love? This is the question that will occupy us throughout these reflections.

A person's marriage is much more important than his line of work, yet most men give much more to the latter. Marriage is a much more fundamental experience in life. If you do not make a success of this basic experience, how can you expect to make a success of other human relationships?

What is a Christian layman? He is someone who takes his task in time seriously and puts all his faith in his life. He is someone who makes something eternal out of the temporal, who tries to make it last forever because he finds it that worthwhile. He is someone who likes what he is doing so much that he wants to keep doing it forever. On this earth you must find something that is worth doing for all eternity; what you begin here will follow you forever. This being the case, you can see how important your love and your homelife are. You have no more important task than to make your love something eternal.

Is it not amazing that we have not gotten around to this question until this century? For the Greeks and Romans love was a touch of madness, a dark demon. In China, societal life was based on the family; but the stabilizing factor was the heritage of past traditions, not love. Even in Europe it was the pressure of institutions that bound people together in marriage. Divorce was taboo, and fear played a part in keeping people together.

This generation—or the next one, for sure—will be the first one in which love alone will keep people together. Previously, people did not necessarily have to love each other to get married. People were glued together; society, the sacraments, and the Church made sure that the glue took hold. Now we can no longer rely on these external pressures. Everything will depend on the couple's love for each other.

Why has it taken the world so long to come around to this point of view? Christianity, for example, is a religion of love; as a matter of fact, it is a religion of incarnate love. Yet marriage has not enjoyed its proper place in the scheme.

Perhaps you have noticed that the Gospel says relatively little about marriage. We find certain elements that seem to cast a positive light on marriage—Christ became man and was extraordinarily human; but other things seem to cast a shadow on marriage—the virgin birth, for example.

Why did the Lord have to be born of a virgin? If God chose to become incarnate, why did he not accept the human way of doing things? The lurking prejudice is clearly brought out in the prevailing confusion between Mary's immaculate conception and Christ's virgin birth.

As you know, these two things are different. The doctrine of the immaculate conception says that Mary was conceived in the usual way, but that from the first moment of her conception she was free of original sin. The doctrine of the virgin birth says that Christ was conceived of Mary but that he did not have a human father. Most people, however, mix the two together: Mary was conceived without sin because she would never have intercourse with a man. You see how the lines get crossed.

One of the Mass texts referring to Mary says, "Without losing the glory of your virginity, you became a mother." I personally would be interested in knowing how women react to this text. What glory is there in virginity when a woman is a mother? What shame is there in becoming a mother the way one usually does? I just do not understand this outlook.

Every Christian home would rest more easy today if Christ had been born of a normal marriage. The only explanation and justification seems to be that in those days people could not have professed Christ's divinity if he had been born in the normal way. God adjusted himself to the outlook of the day, doing what he had to do in order to get through to those people. But that means he adapted himself to their frailty and ignorance. I personally do not see what value you can confer on the miracle itself.

What is virginity? I should hope that for you it is a moral and not a physical quality. There are girls who are virgins without any merit on their own part, and there are other girls who have never been virgins. Even today doctors can tell you of children being born of virgins; the penetration was not complete, and that is all there is to it. But this physiological approach has nothing to do with virginity.

No one is born a virgin. It is something you become, for authentic virginity is chastity. And the measure of your chastity is the extent to which you have spiritualized your sexuality, not the fact of use or non-use. The important question is to what extent you have integrated your sexuality with your love for someone else.

A person who has never performed a sex act may have the vilest and most primitive outlook on sex. Genuine virginity, genuine chastity is a process of educating your instincts to express love. It is not a gift but a process of education.

There has been a truly materialistic cult of virginity in the history of Christianity. Take the famous letter of St. Cyprian regarding virgins. A few virgins had intercourse with deacons, and Cyprian was asked to solve the case. Do you know what he said? "Examine them! . . . see who is still fit for service." Shocking but true! Down and out materialism!

On the tomb of a little seven-year-old girl, Cecilia, they put this inscription: "Cecilia rests in peace, a virgin." That gave her claim to an extra crown. Well, every married woman who truly loves her husband is a virgin. She has a right to every crown there is, for she really won her virginity.

Let me focus on Christ's resurrection for a moment. You all realize, I am sure, that we shall not rise from the dead with the body we had when we were buried. (That is why the Church now permits cremation.) The bowels of the earth are filled with human corpses, and each of us leaves a bit of ourselves to nourish those who come after us. The modern Christian does not believe that the graveyards would suddenly come alive if Christ were to make his second appearance. But in Christ's day, people could not picture resurrection without imagining that corpses would rise from their tombs. It is the way they saw things.

Well, the virgin birth is the same. It is undoubtedly a reality, but the way they looked at it was their own; they focused on

36

the divine value of Christ, not on the value of virginity. Since then we have adopted a materialistic outlook on it. Some theologians say that "Christ passed through Mary's hymen as a ray of sun through a glass"! Is that what the incarnation is?

There is a school of thought about chastity and virginity that really must be challenged. It talks about priests and holy men refraining from tobacco, women, and meat. The three, you see, are put on the same level; they are three ascetic practices. It is a shocking outlook, especially in a religion that preaches love incarnate. We Christians will be judged on our love; the way we love here will follow us into eternity.

What is the message of Christianity? The message of Christianity is that only love is divine and eternal. To put it a little more concretely: God is love. Only love is God, and only love is made eternal. He promised resurrection only to those who love as Christ himself does.

The radically new dimension in Christianity is that God became man. Heaven came to earth, the divine took root in the human, eternity took up life in time. Do you realize that you will live your whole eternity in time, that your eternity will not be the single instant which is God's eternity? You will have a body at the resurrection; and wherever there is a body, there is space and time.

Time is a measure of motion. Wherever there is matter, there we find time. So your eternal life and your eternal happiness will be a human happiness. That is what the resurrection of the body means: it means that your human relationships will be resurrected.

Let me put it another way. The only thing in a creature which corresponds to the infinite perfection of God is its unlimited perfectibility. Your eternal life will be a process of perfecting yourself continually. Hell, for a creature, is the absence of progress. For a creature, hell means staying imperfect and heaven means becoming more perfect.

How horrible it would be if eternal happiness meant immobility for us. How torturous that would be for a living creature, and we shall be alive. Our eternal happiness will involve movement, activity, relationships, and discoveries. God will never cease to be a novelty for us.

How can you tell that you know God? By discovering that you have never known him the way you do now. Well, that is what will happen continually in heaven. And, as far as I can see, you will know him in a human way—that is, through your relationships with other men. The incarnation will still be going on in heaven. Christ will still be incarnate there, and we shall still be trying to flesh out his portrait in every human being we meet there.

Only through your spouse will you come to know God. How does eternity sound to you now? But I am serious. You will know God in a human way. You will come to know the Father through the Son, the Son through the Church, and the Church through your fellow men. You will be resurrected as a man, not as an angel. The resurrection of the body is an essential element of our faith. If Christ did not rise, then our faith is vain.

As I see it, Christianity is the revelation that our eternal life has already begun. If you believe in eternal life, you need only reflect for a moment to realize that it has begun. The worst enemy of Christianity, and of marriage, is belief in some future life—a marvelous future life that will be a holiday from marriage. How many people dream of being widowed for all eternity!

The "life to come" is the opiate of the people because it allows you to look forward to the future without doing anything now. If you are simply waiting for a future life, you are entangled in religious hocus-pocus. I sometimes tell religious, "Don't think that the future life will be a holiday from your community life. It won't be. Your superior will be there. Your fellow religious will be there." You should see the shudders that run through them! They imagine that they will leave all these crosses behind them in this world. And it is the same with a lot of married people. "My God," they say, "will I have to put up with this character in the next life too?"

Eternal life is now. Begin right now to form the kind of relationships that can last forever. Start living that eternal life right now. Many married people think that they will be free of their predicament in another 20 or 30 years, but that is not so. Now is forever, so start changing things today. You must fashion your happiness now. You must start to live now. Separate if you must, but do not stay dead the way you are now.

Is something in your life so good that you want to carry it along for eternity? Have you had moments that you would like to last forever? Do you love someone so much that you want to live with this person forever? I hope so, because that is the only eternity you have. The only thing you can make eternal is your love. Faith and hope will pass away; charity will remain. The things you have loved strongly enough will be carried into eternity with you.

If you were to die tonight, what would you carry into eternity with you? Some people say, "No one and no thing," and think that they are models of detachment. Actually, they are enmeshed in absolute solitude. What do you need? Everything, I hope:

the sky, the sea, the stars, children, books, paintings, music, some special person, everybody. You are furnishing your life in eternity, so get busy on it.

I can think of only one good Christian proverb: Do whatever you want to do, but do one thing that is so good that you would like to do it forever. At first, you begin to think of a thousand things you would like to do: free yourself from all burdens, take a vacation from marriage, etc. But when you focus on the second part of the proverb, you begin to get more cautious. "What would I want to do forever? Well, I think I'd like to be with my wife. If it is to be forever, I'd rather be with her."

The things you do together should be things you would like to keep doing forever. Right now you must make yourself the person you would like to be forever. That and that alone is the purpose and goal of man's life. You will eternalize the things you love enough. Your capacity for redemption is measured by your capacity for love. That is the part of you that will be eternal.

Let me offer a beauty tip to the ladies. You might be wondering what your complexion will be like in eternity. You might be wondering how old you will be at the resurrection. Well, the answer is simple. You will rise with the complexion of your heart; and your age will reflect the vitality of your love.

Consider the risen Christ. He is the only witness we have on this matter. Nobody recognized him at first. He did not reflect their idea of God and, what is more interesting, he did not look like himself any more. But when he began to talk and to do things, people knew it had to be him. He invited his disciples to dinner, he broke bread with them, he called them back to their vocation; he was more himself than ever before, and they could not help but recognize him.

Well, that is how it will be with married people. You will recognize each other in the way you talk and act. You will know that it must be the one you love, more truly yourself than you have ever been.

Only one thing will be resurrected with you: the way you love. That is what your loved ones will recognize. At present your body is as much an obstacle as a means of communication. It casts obscuring shadows as well as clarifying light. At the resurrection, however, you will be transparent; you will radiate the vitality and youthfulness of your love. What else could you possibly bring with you into eternity?

Eternal life is knowing God and the one whom he has sent, Jesus Christ. Eternal life is living a life of love, as Christ does. Only those who live such a life are promised resurrection. If that is the purpose of our life, we must get busy. We must wake from our long slumber at last; we must subject our married life to a thorough-going critique.

CHAPTER 3

The Priesthood of the Laity

At this point I should like to cut across three basic points: the purpose of man's life, the priesthood of the laity, and the notion of community. I should like to start out by citing the text of Luke 22, 14–20.

And when the hour had come, he reclined at table, and the twelve apostles with him. And he said to them: "I have greatly desired to eat this passover with you before I suffer; for I say to you that I will eat of it no more, until it has been fulfilled in the kingdom of God."

And having taken a cup, he gave thanks and said: "Take this and share it among you; for I say to you that I will not drink of the fruit of the vine, until the kingdom of God comes.

And having taken bread, he gave thanks and broke, and gave it to them, saying: "This is my body, which is being given for you; do this in remembrance of me." In like manner he took also the cup after the supper, saying: "This cup is the new covenant in my blood, which shall be shed for you."

I have found much to think about in this text. To begin with, an air of nostalgia surrounds it; Christ looks longingly towards the past and towards the future. It is their last meal together, filled with the melancholy of all such reunions and get-togethers, and Christ looks forward to their future meeting when the kingdom of God comes.

What has struck me most of all is the fact that Christ dedicated three years to building up a community. During those three years he did not celebrate Mass, he did not consecrate anything, he did not even pray with his disciples too much. During those three years, he busied himself with establishing ties of friendship. He tried to fashion a community; it was a pretty shaky community of interested people who had a hard time understanding him aright; they kept asking him for explanations, they bickered over trivial things, they wanted to know who was the most important among them. As they sat down for the Last Supper, they vied for the best seat; so before he sat down, Christ washed their feet.

For three years Christ tried to humanize this group and mold them into a unified community. At the Last Supper he tells them that they are no longer servants but friends. He has established ties of friendship with them and has told them what the Father made known to him.

How did the apostles come to know that Christ was God? I think it happened very unconsciously. They came into contact with him and gradually established ties of friendship. While he was alive on earth, they may never have consciously wondered whether he was God. But he was so honest and loving, so just and friendly, that when he left them they began to examine their attitude towards him. Did they not feel about him as they had always felt about God himself?

There was, to be sure, a moment of crisis in this process. As Jews, they were strict monotheists. It was not easy to accept the fact that there was a God the Son, equal to the Father, or that God had become incarnate. But his deeds made them ponder the whole question: "What manner of man is this, that even the wind and the sea obey him?" Bit by bit they began to see that

43

their attitude towards him resembled their attitude towards God himself.

As a priest, I have often thought about the priestly routine today. We priests say 365 Masses a year, without any community being present most of the time; Christ spent three years trying to fashion a small community, and he said only one Mass. That is a measure of the gap between us. We priests today spend a lot of time trying to sacralize things which do not deserve to be made sacred. We baptize children whose parents have no faith, we marry people who do not love each other, we give the Last Anointing to unconscious people who would send us away if they were conscious. What is all our activity worth?

Christ devoted almost all his time to one main job: fashioning a little community. Is that what you are doing? Can your little community be made sacred? Can your little community be the symbol and the start of something else? Can it be made eternal? Have you created joy together here, which you will be able to drink "anew" in the kingdom of heaven?

Christ and his apostles created something that will reach its full realization in the kingdom of heaven. That is what I was trying to say about your love in the last chapter. But it might be better for you to ponder Christ's words: "I will not drink of the fruit of the vine, until the kingdom of heaven comes."

Do you still want to continue, to begin again? As I see it, marriage is a history shared by two people to a large extent. It is a web of memories, sufferings, conversations, and anxieties that are shared by two people. Indeed, it is sometimes hard to say whether it is a happy thing or a source of suffering; but, at any rate, it is a bond between two people.

I am not sentimental when I talk about love. I think that love is something which creates a common bond and a common history between two people. Nothing ties people together so much as the things they have known and suffered together.

The three years of Christ's apostolate were not an idyllic honeymoon. They were more like married life after the honeymoon is over: "Wicked and perverse generation, how long shall I put up with you?": "You blind men, with hearts slow to believe!" Yet, despite this, certain ties were created that could be carried into eternity. Saddened that he was eating with them for the last time on earth, he looked forward to their meeting in the kingdom of God.

I have often said that the more truly human a thing is, the more truly divine it can become. Christ distinguished an ordinary meal from a sacred one, but he brought them together into an eternal relationship.

We must have something authentically human to make eternal, and herein lies the problem with many marriages today. It seems to me that they are contracted with little real thought. Relishing their freedom at an early age, young people get married before they are really mature. The Church ought to refuse to consecrate their engagement; it should establish a novitiate for marriage, similiar to the catechumenate for baptism. For two or three years the couple should live in a civil marriage; during this period they would be formed and guided in establishing a real home.

I do not mean to deprecate the value of civil marriage nor the sincerity of our young couples. But I do feel that they are not yet capable of the real thing; and the Church has the right, not to pass judgment on their intentions, but to ask for some proof of their determination. The catechumen has faith and wants to be baptized, but the Church requires that he get further instruction so as to become more mature.

"But," you say, "their relations will be so many mortal sins."

That is not true. Conjugal relations are not justified by a green light from the Church. They are justified by the love of the couple and their sincere desire to make a commitment to each other. The catechumen who dies before baptism is saved. The catechumen in marriage who died during his time of testing would likewise be vindicated.

Today we seem to have only two possibilities: the fleeting glory of an affair or the prison of indissolubility. Is there not a need for some sort of intermediate solution: a *respectable* civil marriage that would represent a serious attempt at understanding and love.

Should not the Church sanctify only a love that has stood the test? Christ spent three years trying to sanctify a community. Is it not sacrilegious to dispense our sacraments to anyone who asks for them, without checking to find out whether their love is modelled after the mutual love between Christ and his Church?

During this testing period, the couple would refrain from pro-creation. After all, do they have the right to bring a child into the world before they can assure him of a proper home?

"Ah," you say, "in that case they will never have children. They will become pure egotists." That is the chance we have to take. Is it not better that they never have children than that they have them too soon and then discover they are egotists? In any case, you must never regard children as the indispensable means of consolidating the marital union. A human being can never be regarded as a means. It is the union of the spouses that is the indispensable condition for the procreation of children.

I can see no loftier goal for human activity than this: to create societies and communities that could well be consecrated and made eternal.

Remember what Our Lord told us: "By their fruits you will know them ... Not everyone who says to me, 'Lord, Lord,' shall enter the kingdom of heaven; but he who does the will of my Father in heaven shall enter the kingdom of heaven" (Mt. 7, 16–21). We cannot put divine worship in one corner of our life; it must be part and parcel of our everyday life as men. The Father's will is that we create communities governed by love, that we bring together the dispersed children of God. All men are God's children, but many are unaware or forgetful of this fact. Christians must remind them of God's summons, of the great things he is accomplishing in them; then they may go about their task —creating a united world, a single eucharistic community that can be made eternal.

Christ does not want us to separate God and man. Even before he came, the prophets linked the world of the sacred with social morality and social justice. They found themselves in an environment where the official priesthood and formal worship was flourishing (as Mass celebrations are today!). Countless animals were sacrificed in the temple at Jerusalem, and the Church's cut was pretty good. The prophets came along and insulted this official priesthood; they said that these sacrifices were worthless in God's eyes. "What care I for the number of your sacrifices? says the Lord. I have had enough of whole-burnt rams and fat of fatlings; in the blood of calves, lambs and goats I find no pleasure. ... Make justice your aim. Redress the wronged. Hear the orphan's plea. Defend the widow" (Is. 1, 11–17).

Do those words have a sharp edge today? There are so many Masses in so many richly appointed churches; but to what effect? Everything seems to be running smoothly; but what if it is running on the wrong track altogether? Is it weaving a meaningful pattern? Is it making anything sacred? Or is it boxing life in one compartment and the sacred in another?

Perhaps the most revolutionary thing Christ did was to feed 5,000 people at the time of Passover. Instead of going to the temple at Jerusalem—a serious religious obligation in that era—he holds a banquet for these people in the desert. The cultic ritual of the temple is replaced by the multiplication of the loaves and fish. It is replaced by an act of sharing, an act of community. Today the Church is still preoccupied with cultic ritual. She spends a great deal of money on her sacred edifices and on her religious ceremonies. If she were to spend one or two years distributing bread and communicating her riches, it would be an action quite as revolutionary as that of Christ himself.

After many acts of sharing, Christ fashioned a sacred community. He said that this entente had far greater repercussions than his disciples realized, that man would live forever within the love it expressed.

Vatican II called your attention to the priesthood of the laity. The priesthood of the laity means that in your life as laymen you consecrate things, you make them sacred. Authentic worship is not restricted to churches; it is exercised in daily life as well. I want you to see clearly that what you are doing in your married life is what you are doing in every phase of your life: creating a community, radiating love, inviting people to unite with each other.

In your life as spouses and parents, you have your first and most important experience at fashioning a community. If you fail there, how can you pretend to succeed elsewhere? Your married love has a universal as well as an eternal aspect. Not only must it be made eternal, it must also be spread to others.

That is what your priesthood means. And, unfortunately, up to now married love has been subordinated to something else.

What does it mean to say that you are priests? Well, a priest is a man of sacrifice. Priesthood and sacrifice go together. Sad to say, we have distorted and twisted the meaning of this word "sacrifice." For us it means immolation, destruction, mortification, loss: "God is a sadist asking us to be masochists."

What does sacrifice really mean? It means "to make something sacred." In other words, it means to give something the highest value it can possibly have, to make the profane sacred. And since only God is sacred and holy, to sacrifice means to divinize something, to fill it with God.

And what is God? God is Love. So to divinize something means to fill it with love. The priesthood of the laity means that you fill the beings around you with love, that you sacrifice them. The most religious act becomes operative in the realm of the profane. There is no greater religious act than calling a being to genuine love because this consecrates and divinizes him. Nothing is more divine than man's activity of loving.

I have often been struck by the paradoxical truth that man can become man only with the help of God, that he must be introduced to himself by another. Not long ago there was an interesting debate among the Catholic intellectuals of France. They were trying to pinpoint the difference between the pagan moral law and the Christian moral law. They could not, because the moral law is based on man's real nature. Christianity does not add a single precept to this basic moral law.

Yet, with the coming of Christ, everything has been changed. Why is this? Well, if you explicitate the basic moral law, you will say that man must develop himself and that he can only do this by listening to others and respecting their rights. Christ introduced a radically new element into the mix: he demonstrated that God has manifested himself in our midst, as the lowliest of all and the servant of all.

The uniform of our God is the apron. He puts on an apron to wait on you at table. He becomes chief cook and bottle-washer. The Almighty becomes a servant and washes your feet. Nothing could be better for you than the shock of seeing your God as a servant. Christian worship involves taking cognizance of the service which God renders to us. It is for this service that we render him thanks. The greatest service we can render to God is to take cognizance of the service he renders to us.

When you submit to this shock, your way of living is radically changed. When you discover that to be God is to love and to render service like that, then your outlook is transformed. We are no longer in the realm of natural morality, we are in the realm of the supernatural. Not only are we to polish our own shoes; we are to polish our neighbor's shoes too! Before Christ, no one could have imagined that this was the secret of happiness; and it is, because God is happiness.

It is strange that God had to reveal this to us, but that is the fact. God showed us something entirely new in the area of human relations. He showed us that there is more happiness in giving than in receiving, that he who would be first must become the lowliest servant of all. That is something we try hard to forget.

Who is the head of the family? The man, it is to be hoped. But what exactly is the role of the head in the Church? His role is to serve, to be the lowliest of all. That is why the wife plays the dominant role in most marriages—because she renders more service. The men of the house should not be discouraged by this fact, they should not relinquish their prerogative, they should strive to serve more! And they should stop pouting about the fact that they are the lords of their castles.

St. Paul made a shocking and wretched remark: "Woman is made for man, and man for Christ, and Christ for God." He had his sociological and environmental prejudices, and they must be distinguished from his inspired pronouncements. Here it was Paul, the man, talking.

We make every effort to forget the happiness which God has revealed to us. The Church became imperious, and she remained that way for a long time. Now, since Vatican II, she is trying to become a poor servant once again. In short, she is trying to rediscover her authentic values, to become Christian once again.

The priestly work of the laity is to put the world in the state of grace. And what does grace mean? It means love, it is a summons to love. To give grace is to give love. I cannot think of anything else for us to do. We have but one goal in life: to fashion a community—or rather, communities—of love.

It is worth noting that Christ used bread and wine for his Eucharist. In other words, he used the plainest and most basic materials of everyday life. Bread symbolizes man's life and work and family existence. The bread which you share at your table is the bread he consecrated. He did not create it specially. He works with our materials.

In this connection, I would urge you to be wary of substitution in religion. Beware of the pinch-hitter! Beware of any god who would substitute for you or take your place in the lineup! For example, you hear someone say, "Christ suffered for us." Take it slow for a moment: that does not mean he suffered in your place; you have to suffer too. Christ did not suffer and die in your place. He suffered and died so that your sufferings and death might be like his: full of love. In other words, Christ respected man and did not do things in place of man. He did things so that man could do them in the same way.

You sometimes hear people say, "The Carmelites and other contemplatives pray in the place of those who do not pray." That is wrong. There is no substitution, no pinch-hitting here. They pray so that those who do not pray will learn how to pray. We have got to work this idea of substitution out of our religion.

Christ did not substitute for us, he did not take our place. It is our bread that he consecrated, our human community that he made sacred and eternal. At the Last Supper he extended a little human community into eternity; in like manner, it is your human relationships that are made sacred.

The bread of the Last Supper is the symbol of all human relationships. Your bread is your family, your job, your relationships in the parish and the community at large. Can you consecrate your bread now, or will you have to make some alterations first? It would be terrible if you made us share a mouldy piece of bread, mildewed with bitterness, deceit, and infidelity. Then again, perhaps your bread is kneaded with love. Perhaps there is something in your human relations that is really worth making eternal. At any rate, that is the question you must ask yourself.

Without bread I cannot say Mass. Yet I celebrate Mass 365 days a year without a community being present. That frightens me, because Christ spent three years fashioning a community before he celebrated any Mass. You, fortunately, do this same kind of work every day of the year. You do not say Mass but you are busy fashioning a community. At least I hope you are trying to fashion a community that I might help make sacred.

There is the connection between the priesthood of the laity and that of the priestly minister.

The great put-on in Christianity is fleeing your family and professional life to a quiet little nook in church. There you think: "Here with God everything is okay. He gives me the patience I need to wait for the life to come." In reality, the only thing God can give you is the courage to knead your daily bread with more love, so that your bread will be worthy of eternal consecration.

Let me put another question to you, so that you will see even more clearly how to relate the sacred to your daily activity. Why do you think Christ chose to share himself in the course of a meal? What connection do you see between this meal and Christ's death?

Many of the old-time preachers have this complaint: "Young priests today talk about Mass as a brotherly banquet, but they no longer talk about sacrifice. The Mass is, first and foremost, the commemoration of the sacrifice on Calvary. At Mass we are by the Cross." What, then, is the connection between sacrifice and breaking bread together in a friendly meal?

There is a fantastic connection between a meal shared together and the sacrifice of one's life. Christ's death was a death suffered out of love, a surrender of his own life for the sake of others. It is very easy to commemorate Christ's death on Calvary in the joyous atmosphere of a brotherly meal.

A meal is a sacrifice. Where do parents teach their children that they love them? Where do children learn this lesson? At the family meal. When the children have grown up and their parents want to experience this family tie once again, what do they do? They invite their children to dinner. The father spends his life trying to earn this meal—that is the thing to remember. All his work outside the home culminates around the dinner table. The family meal is a sensible sign, a sacrament. The children eat and drink the work, the life, the love of their father.

As for the mother, she spends her life preparing these meals. Her whole life, in a way, is spent creating the atmosphere that surrounds the family meals. I do not mean that she actually makes the meals every day. I mean the creation of the surrounding atmosphere is peculiarly her work.

Children eat and drink the life of their parents, the work of their parents, the love of their parents. The children's growth runs parallel with the decline of their parents. You are the living proof that your parents loved you and grew old in the process. You have grown to the extent that you were nourished and loved, both physically and psychologically. And, in the same sense, your parents have completed their life and worn themselves out.

Do you think that this is a sad thing for your parents? Well, it is not. Your parents are overjoyed to see their children eat and grow. It is when children do not eat that their parents are sad.

If this be true, why should anyone want to give the Mass an air of sadness? Christ is delighted when we eat. He is glad to give his life. He is glad to help you grow in love. He fashions a community and consecrates it at a meal. The sacrifice, the joy, the meal, the death on Calvary all go together; they all represent the gift of his life. Do not think that Christ was jealous of his life and miserly about surrendering it. He gave it gladly. "He gave thanks." It was a joy for him.

Now do you begin to see the authentic cast of your Eucharist? It is to be hoped that, out of all your sacrifices, out of all your family meals, out of all your attempts at building communities, you have already created something which Christ can take and make eternal some day. That is your role in this world. I cannot imagine anything more basic or more important. And your professional life, your activity outside the home, should echo this eucharist. If your children have not celebrated your eucharist time and again, they will never understand Christ's Eucharist.

Let me return to our Gospel text for some final thoughts. "The hour had come." Throughout the gospel there is mention of an "hour" towards which Christ is moving. This world does not contain its own justification or its own light. It is a sacrament. Your life, too, is a sacrament; and so is your marriage. It is the sign of something else and the start of something else. It comes from beyond you. It is a call, a vocation, a love that passes through you.

As you know, you are the ministers of the sacrament of matrimony. In other words, the love involved here is much bigger than you, but it passes through you to another. This love is actually far beyond you. To give up one's life for others, to embrace the cross joyfully in order to save others—that kind of love is superhuman. So you are the sign of something that is much greater than you. At the same time you are the start of something: in other words, you must create something which will consecrate and make eternal your lives and the lives of those who spring from you. You, too, are moving towards an "hour."

Christ's hour had come. Your hour will come some day. Do you have something you can make eternal? Have you fashioned enough things with which to furnish your eternity? Do you love enough things to make your eternity a fulfilling experience? Come alive!

Last year I went to Canada. I was delighted to discover that

55

countless people are going back to school. They are being lured back by the siren song of education. The adults outnumber the young people in the university. Evening courses are more crowded than daytime classes. People are spending a couple of nights a week in school to get their bachelor's degree in five years.

It is a fine thing! They are opening their windows to the world outside. They are learning something. And how about you? Are you ready to return to the classroom? Are you ready to learn something new? Are you still educating yourself? Are you still filled with curiosity about what is going on in the world?

Remember: it is now that you choose what you will be doing for all eternity. *The happiness of heaven is a human happiness.*

"I will not drink of the fruit of the vine, until the kingdom of God comes." It is a continuing thing. When you meet God, he is not going to punish or reward you. I hope that you are done with that notion! God is not a policeman, nor is he a judge. If God is simply someone who metes out punishments or rewards, he might as well be replaced by a computer. Then all you would have to do is drop your time-card in the slot and get your payment.

But that is not how God works. God offers you a love that can be made eternal, a life that can be made eternal: his life, his joy, his pleasure. Can you already taste this joy? If you can, then you will go on tasting it forever. God will not punish or reward you, he will make you eternal.

For all eternity you will be doing the things you like to do. And if you do not like what you are doing, or if you are not doing anything, you will be stuck with this for all eternity. To look on God as a watchdog who is keeping tabs on you is a childish and dangerous outlook; for you then begin to expect from him what you should be expecting from yourself.

"And when the hour had come, he reclined at table, and the twelve apostles with him. And he said to them: 'I have greatly desired to eat this passover with you before I suffer. . . .'" Christ is recalling with relish the memory of countless meals shared with his disciples. He is recalling the countless experiences they shared, particularly those that merit being made eternal. Do you remember when they returned from preaching and told him that they had been able to overcome demons? He told them that they should not rejoice over that, that the important thing was that their names were inscribed in heaven. That, you see, was something worth making eternal.

Christ will sup with them again in heaven. For in heaven our earthly activities will be fully realized and made eternal. Here on earth there is something of a shadow between us. We cannot see each other fully. We never manage to say clearly and fully how much we love someone. In heaven, however, we shall. Death opens out on a new world, but it is a world where we shall live the things we have lived here on earth.

"And having taken bread, he gave thanks and broke, and gave it to them, saying: 'This is my body, which is being given for you; do this in remembrance of me.'"

Christ gave thanks, and then gave the bread and wine to his disciples. It is something you have done often at table. Can you make your meals eternal? Can you give thanks that your meals are filled with the same kind of love?

Your family meals are the sacrament of your love. When the woman of the house tries to figure out what she is going to make for supper, she is wondering how she can best show her love. When the man of the house sits down at the table, he sees his life and his work before him on the platter.

"Do this in remembrance of me." It is not a sentimental

banquet, a gesture of nostalgia. His disciples are to continue doing the same thing, to make their meals eternal. And that is what you are to do also.

Christ offers his disciples the cup of "the new covenant." Every Mass is a marriage, because covenant and marriage mean the same thing. Christ restored marriage to its true dignity and made it eternal. Christ made your love an eternal thing. And he did it through his saving love, through his total gift of himself. It took God to introduce man to himself. It took Christ to show us what it means to be human beings: to serve others, to sacrifice oneself for others, to sanctify them, to love them strongly enough to save them. There is no greater happiness than that. And if your love is like that, then you will be able to go on loving for all eternity.

CHAPTER 4

Conjugal Spirituality

By conjugal spirituality I mean the way in which you love each other. It is an important thing, and I should like to get you thinking seriously about it.

I have already discussed the great enemy of marriage and of religious life, routine. But marriage has another enemy that is just as dangerous. That enemy is silence.

When two people get engaged, they talk to each other all the time. They dream dreams, they plan the future, they show inventiveness, they create. And, as I pointed out earlier, such mutual interchanges are necessary to keep love alive. They must not stop.

Now if you ask a married man whether he is doing this, he will say, "Oh, sure." His wife will retort, "Since when?" He is convinced he has, you see, but she has a rather different opinion about that. Needless to say, the situation is reversed in some instances; it is the woman who must check up on herself.

As a general rule, men do not like long explanations. They get to the point quickly and express themselves in their own verbal shorthand. Their work is their outlet and their proof that they love their wives. They "adore" their wives, they idolize them, but they do not talk to them too much.

Unfortunately, a woman is not long satisfied with this silent adoration. She wants to live, to talk, to create, to do things; instead, she is walled up in a silent house.

A man usually is not much of a talker—but I am not trying to say that his wife is therefore a saint. She can do worse still. She can go on talking year after year, all the time saying nothing about what is really essential. To get her talking about the really important things can be like pulling teeth.

When a husband stops talking, it is usually out of laziness; when a wife stops talking, it is usually a deliberate act on her part. A man stops talking because he is negligent; a woman stops talking because she wants to hide something, because it would take too much out of her to say what she really has on her mind. She camouflages her real thoughts behind a flood of words. What she says no longer has any real meaning. The result is a frighteningly complex and confusing state of affairs. The husband finds his wife "baffling" or, when he is really angry, "insincere."

A woman needs someone else to be happy. This is the root of female egotism. A man has his egotism, too, and unfortunately male and female egotism are of different sorts. So each party sees the egotism of the other, but fails to see his or her own egotism. The egotism of the other person seems to be quite unique in this world.

The man is egotistical in that he can be almost fully satisfied by himself alone; he does not need much to be happy. He needs a woman to decorate the house, but she must be content with being an ornament: "Be beautiful and shut up." The woman, on the other hand, is happy only if she can talk to him and share his happiness. Each, therefore, must fight his or her own egotism. The man should pay attention to the woman, and she should be careful not to impose herself too much on him. A woman needs to have someone need her; and in this area of needing each other, we are not always generous.

Let me give you a classic scene. The husband comes home in the evening. He has spent the day working and talking to people; all he wants is peace and quiet. His wife has been home all day; she has been waiting for someone to talk to, for someone who will take her away from the house—mentally if not physically. (It must be physically sometimes, of course.) In short, when they meet in the evening, they are at opposite poles.

Let me suggest a basic precaution. When a man comes home from work in the evening, leave him in peace for at least half an hour. He needs that much time to recuperate from the day, because his work can be traumatic. His wife must rein in her desire to talk to him or to implement her threats against the children ("Wait till daddy comes home!"). He simply is not ready for it.

One day, when I was discussing this matter, a woman said, "We have settled this problem, Father. When my husband comes home from work in the evening, he stays out in the car for a half hour." Well, he has the right idea. He works up enough courage to step inside the door. But it would be even better if she let him do it inside. Then, after the half hour is up, it is he who must make the extra effort.

A man must take his wife out once in a while—say, once every two weeks anyway. He must talk to her and tell her what is going on. If he does not, the consequences could be fatal. I know some women, intelligent women, who look forward to seeing their housekeeper so that they can have someone to talk to. What a pitiful situation!

A woman is intelligent and generous only if she adapts her involvement to her husband's need for it. "Do you want something, dear?" "No, you can see that I'm satisfied." "Do you like that?" "Well, you see I'm eating it, don't you?" "Do you want some more coffee?" "If I wanted some more, I would have asked for it." But of course she must involve herself sometimes; here is where her common sense and good judgment come in.

A woman should know that when a man is not saying anything, he is often thinking. A man keeps quiet when he thinks. A woman talks when she is thinking. That does not hold for either all the time, of course; but the two processes are basically different. So a woman must be wise enough to know when her husband should be left alone and when he should be brought back from himself. It takes a touch of genius.

What about going out together? Obviously, they cannot stay home all the time, and they should not be out all the time either. Here again, a touch of genius is called for. Another classic case: the couple has decided to go out a particular evening. The day comes and he gets home from work a little late. He slumps into a chair, proclaiming how tired he is. She is getting dressed: "You haven't forgotten, have you dear?" "Forgotten what?" "We're going out tonight, remember?" "What are you talking about? When was this decided?" "Last Thursday, remember?" "Oh, yes, now I remember. Listen, honey, why don't you go by yourself? I'm beat!" "No, I'm not going by myself." After much coaxing, she has gotten him to change his clothes and he trudges out the door with her.

Now they are at the party. Suddenly he is wide awake again among his friends and among the pretty young things. His conversation is brilliant, his manners superb, his company a delight! Eventually, she has to drag him home by the ear. Back in the taxi around 2:00 a.m. he slumps down in the seat: "And I have to get up at the crack of dawn!" But she is happy and content. She has aired her pachyderm, and fresh air is circulating through the house once again.

It is terribly difficult for two people really to understand each other. That is why they must talk to each other. If you do not keep on comparing your outlooks on life, if you do not trade ideas with each other, it is all over. Your conversations and even your disputes will cement your relationship. You must talk to understand each other. After the big quarrels come the wonderful reconciliations. And reconciliations are better than absolute silences.

Marriage is a tight line between two precipices: unreasonable demands and total resignation. You must never resign yourself to the present situation, yet you must not be unreasonable in your demands either. You must never completely accept your spouse as he or she seems to be at a particular moment; yet you cannot demand outright that he or she change either. An outright demand will prevent your spouse from changing.

Resignation is not the answer either. You must continue to put your hope in your spouse, you must continue to look forward to what your spouse will be some day in the future.

This brings us to another question: Must you tell your spouse everything that is on your mind? Certainly not, not all at once. You have been silent for such a long time, you are not used to talking. But, on the other hand, if you give up hope of telling each other everything some day, then you are no longer married. If you do not live in the expectation that some day you will finally say and understand everything, then you are no longer married.

There is no doubt that some associations and relationships with people outside the home come more easily and quickly. You must take advantage of these associations to exchange them with your spouse some day. You must always say a little more than you feel like saying, a little more than your spouse may be able to grasp right away. If you do not increase the dose steadily, there will be no progress at all. The conversation of husband and wife must strike a few sparks, it must provoke a further attempt at deeper understanding. If you want to keep cool, to say only nice things, you will not have anything to say.

Moreover, you cannot be demanding. Why? Because if your spouse is to change, you must love him or her. Your spouse must be accepted by you, otherwise there will be no chance to change.

Marriage is a paradoxical situation. The basic pattern of affective motivation is broken deliberately. Ordinarily, we love someone for some quality which deserves our love. This is what you ask of your children when they introduce their betrothed: "Why do you love her?" "Because she has this quality . . ."

In marriage, the whole pattern is turned upside down. You love your spouse and your children, not because they are worthy of it, but in the hope that they will prove worthy of it. If you wait for them to earn your love, you will wait a lifetime. To become worthy of your love, they must be loved *unconditionally*.

Marriage is a commitment to love and be loved unconditionally, whether this love is deserved or not. If you put conditions on your love, it is no longer love. You do not start out by trying to change your spouse; you start out by giving your spouse room for change. Your spouse must be loved so much by you that he or she will find the courage to change. Your marriage must navigate between the twin reefs of resignation and excessive demands. Demands without love will revolt your spouse; love without expectation will degrade your spouse.

Another classic scene: the young bride comes to visit Father. When you have watched young people grow up, they often ask you to marry them. Then, two or three months after the wedding, the glowing young bride comes to pay a courtesy call. "Father, did you get the card I sent on our honeymoon? It was wonderful. I'm so happy!" She talks of this and that and, at the opportune moment, you thank her for the visit and move towards the door.

At that precise moment, her face takes on a serious expression. "Oh, Father, there is something I want to ask you." You take a deep breath and wait. "Father, do you think I should let George become an egotist?" "What a silly question! Of course you should not let George become an egotist." What else is there to say? "Well, you see, this is a real problem for me. George is a wonderful person, very kind, and he loves me very much. But he has no regard for my feelings. If we go to the family for dinner, it is always to his family. If we go out, we always do what he wants to do. Can I let him become that egotistical?"

My first reaction would be to ask her, "Do you think the proper way to handle this is by showing your own egotism? Will that take care of his egotism? Why not give in generously and thus set a pattern for him to imitate?" But she certainly is right: George cannot be left like that forever.

One might spend a great deal of time discussing how to change George; but she certainly should not resign herself to the present situation, deciding that he will never change. Alas, there are characters who give us the impression that they will never change. How do we determine what can and what cannot be changed in them? There are times when it seems to be a dead-end street. In this situation, the words of Christ seem to be particularly apt: "He who seeks to save his life shall lose it, and he who loses his life shall save it."

Your main duty to each other is to keep yourself alive. The husband must remain a dashing Romeo to some extent, he must flirt with his wife and win her time and again. The wife must not use the home or the children as an alibi for giving up her role as a woman. She must set aside moments for recreation, for reading, for studying, and so forth.

Many women play the role of martyr in the home. "After all I've done for you," they say to their husbands and children. The most important thing she must do for them is to keep herself alive, to remain a vibrant woman. To kill herself for their sake would be the worst thing she could do.

Now in this connection we must consider a particular kind of death that is very relevant. It is a feeling we sometimes have that we are somehow dying, that some part of us is fading out. In truth, we sometimes find a better life only by experiencing this taste of death. It is a psychological feeling, you understand, not passive submission to suffocation by another. And even though the end result is a happier life, it is not easy to endure this process of dying. Some of the artificial aspects of life must be sacrificed, if our life is to be lived in its full depth.

Christian ascetism is never a renunciation. It is always a preference. Christ never advised us to kill ourselves. The word "mortification" has become quite popular, but its real meaning has become obscure. To "mortify" is to "put to death," but Christ never told us to put ourselves to death. He told us to mortify our pride, our anger, our jealousy, our faults. Christian ascetism is a preference. We must find something better before we give up what we have. The man who finds a treasure in a field can go off and sell what he has to get that field. The man who has found a precious pearl can sell the pearls he has. But if you have not found that treasure or that pearl, keep what you have; you will pay dearly if you do not.

You serve your wife in that you disengage yourself from other women. You serve your husband in that you reserve yourself for him alone. It is a preference you make and, in that sense, it is a renunciation.

One could make up a little homily for married people that would parallel the kind addressed to nuns at their profession: "I congratulate you, my friend, because you have chosen a narrow and difficult road. To a world which rejects sacrifice for the sake of pleasure, you offer an example of renunciation. You have renounced others for the sake of your spouse. You have said goodbye to others and embraced this cross as your own."

Why should we congratulate a person who gives up what he has for the sake of a treasure? Because Christian renunciation always involves a preference for something better. We willingly agree to undergo the feeling of death because we seek a better life. But husbands and wives cannot sacrifice themselves to each other for the wrong reason.

Recently I gave a retreat to college girls. Marriage lay in the near future for many of them. I explained to them that a woman today must keep a window open on the world; to be a person she must have some occupation, in the broad sense of that word, because family life today is different than it used to be. People live in apartments, have many conveniences at their fingertips, and generally have smaller families. A woman's work as housewife is not enough to provide her with full scope for creativity.

I then posed this question: "If you had to give up one of these things—your profession, your marriage, or your motherhood—which would you sacrifice?" Almost all gave the same answer: "My professional work. I would readily sacrifice my work for my marriage." What a shocking answer! How can you even think of giving up your work for the sake of your marriage? It is unthinkable that you would sacrifice any one of these things for the other. What you must do is integrate all three. If your husband truly loves you, then he wants you to grow as a person and a woman, to develop your capacity for creative work. Otherwise, he is merely looking for an ornament to hang up in his home, and you are it!

No one has the right to let himself die for the sake of another. The children, of course, may keep mother home for a number of years; they are entitled to have a mother. But a child only needs his mother for about four years; after that he goes to school, and he profits more from being with his peer group than he does from being with his mother. If you have four or five children, that adds up to about 15 or 20 years. Once upon a time people began to prepare for death at the age of 40. Today you still have 30 years in front of you. What are you going to occupy yourself with for those 30 years? I certainly hope that you are not going to rest content with hanging around your husband; that just is not enough.

When is it permissible to die for someone? Never. But sometimes we can experience the *feeling* that we are dying. It happens frequently between 35 and 40, in every walk of life. You wake up one morning and you see your spouse beside you: "How could I have married this person? Where did these kids come from? I must have been in a trance all this time." Life is a series of progressive maturations.

At what age will you truly be yourself? At what age will you be able to make a really worthwhile choice? The great temptation in marriage, and it is a noble one in many ways, occurs when a person suddenly says to himself: "I have never really lived, I have never really been myself. Up to now I did not know who I really was." We must be prepared to answer that question when it pops into our head; we must start preparing our response now.

One day we suddenly find someone to whom we can relate quite spontaneously and vitally. When our spouse has become a bit dulled, this new encounter seems to be a re-creation; life has new zest for us, and we wonder how we can give up this new-found vitality.

The best solution for this dilemma seems to be prevention. Do not let it happen in the first place. You must spare each other from this temptation by keeping your love alive always. You might also look at it this way: Granted that this new encounter has added new zest to your life, did you not go through this same experience when you were courting your spouse? Is your life going to be a series of endless courtships, one after the other, with no probing to the innermost depths? Is it not true that you can only probe the depths with the person you chose to marry?

The sole purpose of marriage is to enable you to live all the love of which you are capable. Some people will give you a superficial feeling of vitality; but only your spouse, the person you chose to marry, can ask this much of you. Marriage, as I see it, summons us to love actively all the time; that is the obligation it sets before us. Your spouse and your children are the means whereby you summon up all the love of which you are capable—more love than you thought you were capable of. Therein lies the great difference between married people and celibates.

I once gave a retreat to unmarried men and women, and the problems of celibacy were discussed freely. Sexual frustration was considered, of course; it is a difficult thing, but it can be borne. The women present stressed the emotional loneliness and frustration: "You don't have anyone to talk to, to confide in." I assured them that I often hear the same complaint from married women; they all are looking in vain for a man who will talk to them. Mauriac tells the story of an old Jesuit who is besieged with a flock of pretty young penitents, to the thorough amazement of those around him. What is his secret? Mauriac puts it simply: "He listens to them." Can you imagine the depths of silence in their homes that drive them to this old man?

We continued to talk about celibacy. The great danger in celibacy, it seemed, was that a person might never become a real adult. One could grow old without ever growing up. One could cater to one's whims for a whole lifetime, opting out of a job or any situation when it starts to put demands on him. The celibate can become an adult only if he finds something absorbing and demanding enough to summon up his best effort. The celibate must find something as demanding as a spouse, as time-consuming as children.

A spouse or a child is someone against whom there is no defense, no protective barrier. The celibate has all kinds of defensive barriers. To become a parent is to begin to be vulnerable, to shed one's defenses and accept suffering for the sake of a spouse or a child.

The celibate wears protective blinders. Needless to say, so do many married people; they are celibates out of place. The married person who really fulfills his role stays open and vulnerable. He is irritating and irritable; in other words, he is capable of stimulus and response. The squabbles are a good sign, because they show that there is still contact between the couple. Silence is the symptom of hopelessness and lost love.

In the last analysis, everyone's vocation mirrors that of St. Peter:

" 'Amen, amen, I say to thee, when thou wast young thou didst gird thyself and walk where thou wouldst. But when thou art old thou wilt stretch forth thy hands, and another will gird thee, and lead thee where thou wouldst not.' Now this he said to signify by what manner of death he should glorify God." (Jn 21, 18–19)

When we are young we go where we want to go and we do what we want to do. So we have a yardstick for measuring our maturity. We are adult to the extent that we have been led beyond the point we had planned to go. The married person puts his hand in the hands of his spouse and his children. He accepts vulnerability and suffering. That is what it means to be a spouse and a parent.

When this first happens, you have the feeling that you are dying. But when you look back on the road you have taken, you are content with having made the journey. You would not have chosen it on your own, but you are glad to have made it. Your experience is the same as St. Peter's.

Remember what happened on Mount Tabor at the time of the Transfiguration. Peter was in ecstasy and wanted to build a memorial, but Christ told him to say nothing about it before his passion and death. When Peter was crucified, head downward, he probably uttered a sigh of content over the journey he had made from Tabor to the cross.

So it is with the married person. When he gets married, he makes all sorts of enthusiastic promises. And like Peter, he scoffs at the notion of suffering. Time goes by, the sufferings come; and when it is all over, he is glad to have made his way through it all.

After Christ told Peter what would happen to him, he said, "Follow me." Remember he said the same thing to the rich young man, who had been very faithful in keeping the commandments. When the young man asked for some commandment or credo, Christ simply said, "Follow me." In other words, he told the rich young man to enter a *personal relationship* with him. It is a very important point.

The whole New Testament is a love relationship. Christianity is a religion of love, a religion that tells us to have a personal relationship. Christ did not give his apostles a body of doctrine or an organizational plan. He told them to follow him, and he promised them the Holy Spirit. When he was gone, they would have a personal relationship with his Spirit. And so it is with every Christian. He is to have a personal relationship with the Spirit, he is to deepen his relationships with other men, and he is to be led along a road he cannot foresee in advance.

This is the choice that confronts us: to live on the surface of life or to explore our personal relationships in depth. Husband and wife must love each other unconditionally, must give each other room to grow, must wait for the infinite reaches of their individual personalities to flower. Each must take the other by the hand along an unglimpsed road, developing the undreamed-of potential of that other being. That is the power which you have over each other and, in exercising it, you will know that you are one.

It is in using this power that you know you are truly married. You come to know each other, you come to know yourselves, as you fashion and create each other. The sufferings and the experiences you have shared bind you together. Most and best of all, however, it is the process of mutual creation that ties you into oneness.

CHAPTER 5

Adult Love

So far I have tried to explain the nature and importance of love in human life. Now I should like to talk about adult love. The word "adult" is used a great deal today. We talk about the adult Christian, the adult layman. But what does "adult" mean?

There are countless definitions for the word. As you may know, psychologists claim that 60 per cent of the people never go beyond the mental maturity of a twelve-year-old, and that 30 per cent never get beyond the maturity of a three-year-old. I do not find this hard to believe. But even more important, I think, is the notion that various parts of our being stop growing at different points. We are twelve-year-olds in some respects, and twenty-year-olds in other respects. In short, the problem is that we are not integrated adults with fully matured personalities.

The growth process moves by fits and starts. There are times when we leap forward, and times when we regress. I should like briefly to examine a few stages in the process, so that we can talk more intelligently about this whole question.

At the age of three, the child is a real conservative. He is afraid of change and innovation because he needs a stable world. He performs routine activities over and over again. He becomes aggressive and anxiety-ridden when someone tries to alter his behavior pattern. A good portion of the population could be classed in this category.

At twelve, the child seems incapable of seeing reality as it is. He builds castles in Spain, he dreams of transforming the whole world. Every six months he has a new hero and a new cause to champion; but somehow no practical action is taken, and hero succeeds hero. It is a course taken by many people. They do not build on their past; they continually substitute one thing for another without building anything. They do not use their past; they just keep replacing it.

The fifteen to sixteen-year-old looks for some abstract truth. It is an impersonal truth, lacking a certain human touch. He is hung up with ivory-tower reasoning, because he finds it difficult to master his emotions and hence avoids emotional commitment. Ashamed of his inner turmoil, he tries to act cool. He draws a shell around himself so that he can move about without getting hurt. He hangs around with other kids, rubbing shell to shell and avoiding the risks of openness. He is sad and troubled, and yet he basks in this sadness because it heightens his individuality. When he is melancholy, he can feel his self squirming uneasily within.

Then suddenly, at some point, the teenager runs into someone who dares to be vulnerable. For the first time he catches a glimpse of adulthood, of the power one can wield when one opens oneself to risk, to frailty, to failure. He is forced to re-examine things, and the road to adulthood begins to open up.

As the individual approaches adulthood, he no longer sees life as an either-or choice. He now sees himself as both strong and weak, intelligent and ignorant, good and bad. The world is streaked with goodness and evil, happiness and misfortune.

Maturity is measured by our ability to spring back from failure, to realize that we have to be willing to risk all for something worthwhile. In marriage this means we must avoid shackling our spouse, we must run the risk of losing this person if we are to keep him or her.

Truly adult love involves overcoming indifference, distaste, and deception. Like faith, it is a doubt that we have surmounted. If you have never had doubts about your faith, it is impossible to tell whether you have faith. It simply means that your ideas have jelled with those of the environment around you. Whether you believe in God or simply yourself is an open question in such a case. It is only when God no longer seems to live up to the divine image which you have fashioned that you have a chance to make a real act of faith. Only then do you have a chance to put your trust in him.

As I pointed out earlier, you must have enough light to get through the periods of darkness. But it is in the periods of darkness that you find out whether you really do believe in him. It is then that you verify your real knowledge of him. A child claps his hands when everything is light, and he cries when the darkness comes. An adult clings to his knowledge of the light when the periods of darkness come. To go through life as an adult means to move from light to light *through tunnels of darkness.*

Guardini says that "faith is the capacity to bear with one's doubts." It is, in short, a mature and courageous attitude. To put it another way, faith means having enough light to bear the darkness when it comes. You will always have enough light to bear the darkness; you will always have enough darkness to be tempted to reject the light. Faith, and love, are a call to maturity.

Whether your faith and your love will be tinged with doubt or generosity is up to you. The motives for losing your faith or your love will always be there.

If a man says that his wife has everything, that she is perfect, then I immediately think that he has never really looked at her. Or else it means that he cannot really take her as she is, so he makes up fantasies. It is a common thing, and a bad sign.

When a man says that his wife has many faults but he still loves her, then I know I am talking to an adult. He has enough love to put up with her faults.

That is what love is: a dissatisfaction surmounted. If a married couple are totally delighted with each other, it is hard to tell whether they love each other or simply their own pleasure. Only when a trace of disaffection sets in can we test the real quality of their love. Only then can they exhibit a real act of love. When you think that your love is dying, then you have a chance really to show your love. We must wait to discover our dislikes before we can really know whether we love or not.

Love always involves suffering and struggle. It is an evolving epic, a continuing history. When we love, we agree to be vulnerable. If a husband and wife are not celibates at heart, they choose to share and to communicate with all the risks entailed.

That is the lesson of the wedding feast at Cana. On the very day of their wedding, this couple find out that their resources are exhausted. (This usually takes several years in most marriages.) And it is at that point that Jesus works a miracle, that he resurrects their hopes and their fortunes.

What is the advantage, the fruit, of marriage as a sacrament? Does it give you some grace which the non-Christian does not enjoy? I do not think so. The only advantage of marriage as a sacrament, and it is an important advantage, is that you take full cognizance of your commitment in all its dimensions. Let me explain this point.

God offers his grace to all. God wants to give us much more than we are willing to take from him. He communicates himself to man to the full extent that man opens himself to God. The amount of grace you receive in matrimony does not depend on where it takes place—the church or city hall. It depends on the disposition of the person getting married.

The Christian who gets married has the immense advantage of knowing what real love is and what he can expect in marriage —thanks to Christ. He worships a God who continues to show love on the cross. He knows that love can surmount all obstacles; he rejoices to know that he can save those he loves. This cognizance of the full dimensions of marriage is the only sacramental contribution to your wedding. But, insofar as you have this cognizance, you acquire the proper disposition to receive the grace which comes to those who truly love.

To put it another way: grace increases through prayer and through our actions. A sacrament is both a prayer and an action. And since it is the action of Christ himself, it is a very special type of action; it is the action of him who is love itself.

When you seek to be married by the Church, you are asking that your union be identified with the union between Christ and his Church. Each partner is both Christ and the Church, saving their spouse and being saved by their spouse. Nothing could be more open to grace than this disposition, for it is the disposition of Christ himself.

The real difference between the Christian and the non-believer is a matter of awareness. The Christian knows what he is doing, where he is going, and why. The non-believer knows he should be faithful to his love; but he has not been conformed to Christ, so he is not so well prepared to live his love.

Remember this: it is not some vague, abstract idea about Christ that differentiates the Christian from the non-believer. It is Christ himself—a concrete, living being. As I see it, Christ is not only the most perfect person in the world but also the most real and present person. This living being, whose experience we can participate in, is the basis for Christian marriage. We can come to know and love him, and we can finally let him take over our lives. It is he who should live your marriage; it is his love that you should echo in your marriage. That is what the sacrament of marriage is—not mysticism but a real experience shared with Christ.

When Christ stepped in at the wedding feast, what happened? The water was turned into wine, and the second wine was better than the first. There you have the most beautiful lesson about marriage: the second love in marriage is better than the first.

In the first blush of love, we have an unrestrained enthusiasm. Everything is wonderful. There is no trace of sadness or suffering anywhere to be seen. It is the same way when a young man enters the seminary. He is going to convert the world. The pope and his bishops are geniuses. All sorts of illusions, you see, which probably are not too deplorable at this stage of the game. But what happens when the magic carpet starts to fall towards the ground?

The *second* love is the important one. It is at this point that we love someone else instead of ourselves. It is a love which can put up with difficulties and defects, a love which is willing to accept suffering. This love summons all the resources within us and taxes every ounce of our strength. This is the love which makes adults out of us. And there may well be a third, a fourth, and a fifth love too.

Life is not worth living if you do not stay alive. Marriage is not worth the trouble if you do not keep discovering each other continually. If you think you know your spouse, you had better start trying to get to know her once again. Marriage succeeds only if you start over again time and again, making new discoveries and never being content with the knowledge you have.

When Christ concocted a second batch of wine, everyone was amazed. You must communicate this same feeling of amazement to your children and those around you. If your children are not constantly amazed by your love for each other, if they are not in awe at the way your love grows, then you have not really taught them anything. If you do not teach them anything else, you must teach them that adulthood is a life worth living. You must stay alive and in love your whole life, or they will have no desire to grow up.

Periods of intense growth are always periods of crisis. We suddenly have a doubt about our faith and we wonder if we still believe at all; this is the moment when our faith can really grow into something. And so it is with love.

We could, of course, throw over everything when such moments come. But if we know the way faith and love work, we know that they are infinitely resourceful. We know that dark moments will come and that they can be surmounted. We know that a continual process of growth is involved.

So now let me suggest some questions with which to test your level of maturity. Let me begin by asking you what you would do right now, if you could do anything you wanted to do.

If you are a child, you will look around for something other than what you are doing now. If you are an adult, you will stick with what you are doing now. The adult dreams about what he is doing, the child dreams of something else. The adult applies his thought and imagination to his present work, the child yearns for a vacation from it all.

If you could be anyone you wanted to be, who would you choose to be? The person I am, says the adult. That does not mean he rests content with himself as he is, but that he accepts this person as a starting point. The adult has the courage to accept himself and to work from there. The romantic dreams of changing himself and the world completely, but never seems to get started on either.

Who is responsible for the way you are right now? Here again the real adult answers quite readily, even though it is a hard thing to admit: I myself am responsible for the way I am. I am the product of my own deeds, the fruit of my own labors. I am exactly what I have chosen to be.

This may seem a bit far-fetched at first. But ask yourself this question: Is there anyone who really wants to be someone other than the person he is? Oh, we sometimes say things to that effect, but I really do not know anyone who would change places with someone else. We are exactly what we like to be. Only when we start from that premise can we change the situation we are in. To dream about being someone else is to choke off that possibility of bettering ourselves. We must start from where we are, accept responsibility for our condition, and then do something to better ourselves. Our real situation in life tells us what we have chosen to be.

Remember the words of Jesus: "Everything hidden must be

made known. What you have whispered in secret must be preached from the housetops." So it is with us. The secret desires of our hearts will come to light in our actions; we shall become the being we desire to be. The person we are is a projection of our inner desires.

When a child looks in the mirror, he tries to pretend that the image he sees is not himself. An adult admits that the image is his, and that he is responsible for it. Only insofar as he takes responsibility for his failures can he do something to change the situation. He cannot place the blame on his parents or his circumstances.

Another question to ask yourself: Am I responsible for others as well as for myself? The adult answers "yes." He admits that if he were a better person, others might be better too; that if his love for them were stronger, they too might be more capable of love.

This admission comes much harder. But we must realize how much it enhances our freedom and our capabilities. If we are not responsible for others, there is nothing we can do to change them. But if we do bear responsibility for them, then we can really do something to change them. As Archimedes said, "Give me a place to stand, and I can move the world."

Apropos of this point, I remember a woman who used to get migraines from the loud talk of her children. One day I got a letter from her, informing me that she had almost lost her voice and that now her children rarely talked above a whisper. She found the situation amusing, but she did not realize what was going on. The children shouted because she herself shouted. Now they whispered because she spoke in a whisper.

It is an object lesson for us. If your children are nervous and on edge, calm down yourself. If you want to change your children or your spouse, change yourself first. If you want to change things around you, you must first change things within yourself. Other people and the world outside are a reflection and projection of your own inner state, of your love or your selfishness. It is the thoughts of your own heart that the world shouts from the house-tops. If you want to be an adult, you must recognize your influence and impact on the world around you.

One final question: Which would you prefer, to love someone who does not love you, or to be loved by someone whom you do not love? Your first reaction to this question is probably one of annoyance: "That's an impossible choice. I want to love someone who loves me in return." But, alas, such perfect reciprocity is not to be found. No matter how much unity there is in a home, the love relationship is not one of perfect reciprocity.

One of the great difficulties a woman faces is the realization that a man does not love in the same way that a woman does. A truly adult woman realizes that a man cannot love a woman the way a woman loves a man. She comes to accept this fact, but it is not easy for her to do. It is very hard to recognize and accept the love of another being, when that being does not speak in the same language as you do. Gradually true lovers learn to speak each other's language to some extent, despite the difficulties involved.

The miracle wrought by the Holy Spirit, the miracle of Pentecost, has nothing to do with Berlitz. It did not empower people to speak every language there is, it empowered them to speak each other's language. Thanks to the Holy Spirit, wife and husband can speak each other's language; thanks to the Holy Spirit, both can speak the language of their children;

thanks to the Holy Spirit, clergy and laity can speak each other's language.

Even the most intelligent woman in the world cannot know her husband loves her, if he does not tell her so. And yet men hate to talk, because they find it tiring. They tell their wife of their love by being faithful, by going to work, by coming home in the evening, by putting the house in her name; yet she does not get the point unless he actually tells her that he loves her.

You simply must realize that you are not going to be loved in the same way you love. It is an impossible wish. Man and woman are in different worlds to a certain extent, and this causes each a certain feeling of frustration. But I am afraid that is the way it is with love.

Think back on your own life. Do you not sometimes feel that you are not fully accepted for what you are, that you are not given full room for growth? I think we all encounter patches of obscurity and misunderstanding, and we spend our time complaining about them. But that is the way it is.

Remember what I said earlier about heaven. The only thing that corresponds to the infinite perfection of God is the infinite perfectibility of the creature. This means that we shall be perpetually on the move in heaven, learning something new all the time. We shall never be perfect, but we shall never cease moving towards it. Well, it is the same with love, for God is Love. Our love must move forward continually through a web of surrounding obstacles, with all the suffering that entails.

Like the turtle, we spend much of our time in our own protective shell. To grow, however, we must take risks. We must come out of our shell and expose ourselves to the elements. With each exposure we shall experience a new feeling of happiness and secrete, as it were, a new shell. Then, when we want to grow still more, we shall have to leave that shell and start all over again. That is the way it is with love. To be an adult, we must love someone even if this person does not love us in the same way. Like every mother, we must love without expecting the same in return. We must put our trust in someone and allow this person to grow, hoping that our action will awaken a spark of love in return.

Modern psychoanalysis, which has been much maligned, contains an extraordinarily Christian doctrine. It tells us that to become truly human we must move beyond the state of infantilism, where we get without giving, to a state of self-offering, where we give love even if we do not get it in return. Nothing could be more Christian! And, alas, there really are times when we regress. We yearn to return to the womb, to be loved and protected without having any demands put upon us. Then we get up new courage and we dare to love all over again. So it goes throughout our life.

I remember reading a story about a young man who loved a brilliant concert pianist. He brooded disconsolately because she did not love him. Then suddenly he realized that he was the lucky one, the happy one. He loved someone, and his life had new meaning. He had become an adult, capable of giving love.

There is a note of universality in that kind of love. When a person begins to love like that, he begins to realize that it is possible to love everyone and anyone. In short, the love which you have for your spouse can be developed to cover the whole world. That may sound surprising at first, but think about it for a minute. I am convinced that the motives which kept you faithful to this particular man or woman are the motives which

85

would have kept you faithful to any man or woman. In loving this particular person, you have plumbed the possibilities of love within yourself, and they could have been applied to anyone. It is just that you selected this person at the outset, that this particular person was the one who drew all this from you, that no one else could have taught you this lesson quite so well.

Let me take this point from a different angle. I am convinced that parents love their own children for the very same reasons they would have loved any child. In the beginning, of course, you love your children because they are yours. You even like their faults, and this can become a dangerous thing. But as time goes on, your children change and grow. To keep on loving them, you must draw upon all the resources of which your love is capable. And this same love could have gone to any child.

But all this takes time to learn. You must be led by the hand as St. Peter was. You must come to appreciate what authentic love is. In the confines of your marriage you experience the redemptive love of Christ, and you learn what true love is.

It is said that Christ would have become man even if there had been only one man or woman in the world. It is true, because love is not measured in terms of numbers. His love is the same, no matter how many people are involved. If you had been the only person in the world, he would have suffered the same passion. When you begin to love someone with that kind of love, you will begin to comprehend the love which God has for the whole world. You will realize the intensity of his love, and your love will begin to take on more universal dimensions. When others talk about this love, you will know what they mean.

CHAPTER 6

Women in Today's World

Let me start out by making a provocative statement, so that you will give this whole question some thought: In our culture, women are adult but unhappy, while men are happy but childish. There is a positive correlation between happiness and childishness in the male population.

The most glaring evils around us are the ones that go unnoticed. We are aware of racial and social discrimination, but we take sexual discrimination for granted. We find a pretty young girl going to medical school and meeting rebuffs from the male students, because they feel she is infringing on their domain. Sexual discrimination! We still find Catholic schools debating the ethics of co-education. While some Protestant Churches have accepted the possibility of female clergymen, the Catholic Church has solemnly rejected the possibility of women becoming priests.

If you bring up this latter question at a gathering, it is interesting to watch the various reactions. You can see some of the men pondering this potential new field for seduction, and you can see the women turning up their noses in disgust. Nothing matches a woman's scorn—for another woman. But the fact remains that there is much discrimination against women in society and in the Church.

I remember preaching an Ash Wednesday sermon not too long ago. When I had finished, the master of ceremonies announced that the men present could ascend to the altar and get ashes from the presiding bishop; the women were to get their ashes along the railings of the side altars. It was as if he were separating the sheep from the goats.

In my diocese women are strictly forbidden to be readers or commentators at the Mass. It would be scandalous if they did, I guess. "Let women keep quiet in church" seems to be the guiding norm. They seem to talk so much that someone along the way decided to call them to order. The fact is, however, that even St. Paul talks about women prophesying. The Acts of the Apostles talks about a man who had four daughters that were prophetesses. Just imagine: they could prophesy at home, but they had to keep quiet in church.

While I am on this point, I must say a few words about St. Paul's view of women. We must remember that he was a man of his times in addition to being an apostle. His attitude towards women was very much influenced by prevailing cultural ideas and, unfortunately, this attitude is still the basis for much of the Church's doctrine about women.

I should like to read a few passages from St. Paul (1 Cor. 11, 2–16) and comment on them, hoping that this will be enough to set your teeth on edge:

> "I praise you because you bear in mind all that I taught you and cling to the traditions precisely as I passed them on to you."

Let us see what these traditions are.

"I want you to know, however, that Christ is the head of every man, man is the head of woman, and God is the head of Christ."

But what precisely does that mean in Christianity?

"Every man that prays, or speaks under inspiration, with his head covered brings shame on his head."

So any man who prays or prophesies with his hat on dishonors his head? Well, in China, it is just the opposite. If you are performing a sacred act, you show your respect by putting on a hat.

"Every woman that prays, or speaks under inspiration, with her head uncovered brings shame on her head."

She can prophesy but she must wear a hat! Why? Well here is his first reason why a woman should not have an uncovered head:

"It really amounts to the same thing as shaving her head."

In those days, it was a mark of shame for a woman to have her head shaved or her hair cut short. Haltingly and uneasily, Paul tries to press his rather unconvincing argument.

"If a woman does not cover her head, then she should shave her head. But if it is a mark of infamy for a woman to shave her head or cut her hair short, she should wear a veil."

He senses that his argument is floundering, so he tries to give other reasons. He is obviously not content with the forcefulness of his argument. But he continues:

> "*A man, indeed, must not veil his head, because he is the image and glory of God, but woman is the glory of man.*"

Again he is unsure of himself, so he adds:

> "*Why? Because man did not spring from woman but woman from man. The man, in fact, was created not for the woman's sake, but the woman for the man's sake.*"

The two creation accounts we have in Genesis do not support this interpretation. In one account, both man and woman were created simultaneously. In the other account, they are created at different times; but it is obvious that they are equal. Paul himself quickly interjects another argument, out of thin air it seems.

> "*That is why the women should have a symbol of authority on their head, because of the angels.*"

Is everything clear so far? Well, for a moment Paul seems to get back on the right track.

> "*Yet woman is not independent of man and man is not independent of woman in the Lord. Just as the first woman was drawn from the first man, so man is born of woman. And all things have their origin in God.*"

90

He has admitted that much, you see. But off he goes again:

"Judge for yourselves: is it proper for a woman to pray unveiled to God? Does not nature itself teach you that for a man to wear his hair long is an ignominy for him, and that for a woman to wear her hair long is a glory for her, because her hair was given to her as a covering?"

All this talk of "nature." It seems as if we are back talking about birth control, does it not? And now comes his clincher:

"But if anyone wants to pick flaws in my argument, neither we nor the congregations of God have any such custom."

Well, that settles it. Any questions?

St. Paul obviously was a man of his time and a bit of a misogynist. So we must carefully distinguish the Lord's message from Paul's own time-conditioned ideas. Many theologians have failed to do this, and they will have some embarrassing moments before the throne of God. Suppose God asks them if they ever gave thanks for his first act of love and mercy: giving woman to man because it was not good for him to be alone.

The worst thing about the present status of women, however, is the fact that most women are still not aware of it. In some countries women have pushed for their rights and made great gains, while in other places their situation is hopeless. In Europe especially, little thought has been given to the condition of woman as a whole.

Yet if we are witnessing a great revolution in our day, we

are not really doing anything about it. The revolution is the changing role of woman in present-day society. Today the woman's role in the home is not the active, creative role it once was. In olden days the home was a little universe unto itself. It was a restaurant, a hotel, a cultural center, a nursery, a bakery, a clothes factory. Managing a home took a wide variety of talents and administrative skills.

Today most of these domestic skills have been taken over by men. They are the cooks, the bakers, the hair-dressers, to whom the women go. The modern apartment provides all sorts of mechanical conveniences that reduce the woman's work. It is estimated that the American housewife spends two hours a week shopping. She hops in the car on Saturday and drives to the shopping center. She pays to have the order delivered. In about two hours she has stocked up for the week. In Belgium, a housewife spends about eight or ten hours to do her weekly shopping. Preparing meals should take about 90 minutes a day. If you want a really lavish affair, you go to a restaurant.

And what about child-rearing? Here again the situation of women has changed greatly. To begin with, families are smaller. Today the average married woman has four or five children. The children need her until they are four or five, then the schools take over. That leaves mama with four or five hours a day to herself even when they are small; and 20 years later the children will not need her at all. She will have 30 or 40 years to fill with some sort of activity.

Now we must begin to develop part-time work for women. One of the shocking things about our educational system is that women, who make excellent teachers, cannot work part-time. Even more shocking is the fact that most women have not yet protested against this system. They either teach full-time or do not teach at all. But a woman should be able to teach for a few hours each week. She should be allowed to keep her window open on the world, to develop the talents she possesses.

Today no one can be a real person if he or she does not have some line of work outside his family life. Why? Because family chores have become routine, mechanical, and minimal. The greatest lesson a mother can teach her children today is that she can go on creating and growing as a person even after she has borne and reared them, that she can give to other children the benefits which she has showered on them in the home.

Another urgent necessity is that full-time work for women be geared to their needs and necessities. A woman should be allowed three or four days off a month, just because she is a woman. Something like this has already been set up in Germany. Women should organize to study their problems and to press for their rights in today's world. They should make sure that working conditions are improved to suit the needs of women. Now some may say that all this would be dangerous, because women tend to become entirely wrapped up in what they are doing. But the same is true of men. Many men get completely wrapped up in their work, and they use this as an excuse for ceasing to be alive in other respects. Too lazy to be a whole person, they work like dogs at their profession.

But the major problem is not, in my opinion, giving women the chance to work outside the home. This problem is solved to a large extent, except in the most backward areas. The major problem is allowing women to work *in a feminine way,* to make them professionals without turning them into men. One of the problems of colonialization is that the colonized nation often adopts and exaggerates the faults of the colonizers. Women, who have been under the heel of men for so long, often tend to become too masculine in their work, to lose their femininity. The world of business is a man's world, and it may de-feminize the women who enter it. Considering how much havoc it has wreaked on men, we can well imagine what it might do to women if it were left unchanged.

Now let me make one thing clear. As you can see, I am very much in favor of women having work outside the home. But I do not think they should be compelled to work outside the home. It should be entirely up to them. A woman who keeps house and raises a family should always be held in high respect. Indeed, she should be paid for doing this work, because in our present-day culture the pay-check is our way of showing respect for someone's work. Perhaps the government should pay housewives for their work, even if this means cutting the salaries of their husbands.

The big difference between men and women seems to be their outlook on life: the way they approach life, the way they tackle it, and the way they appreciate it. When a man scents he is near his goal, he hastens forward to grasp it. When a woman scents her goal, she slows down and enjoys the moment. When a man looks at you, he gives you a thorough scrutiny. When a woman looks at you, she lets her gaze play over you; she invents you, as it were.

I mentioned earlier that outside the home men seem to be quite happy while women do not, and that inside the home women seem to be happy while men seem to get bored. Let me try to offer some explanation for this phenomenon.

I think men are basically simple, uncomplicated creatures. A man is readily content with what he has, and he quickly adapts himself to what he is doing. If he goes into business, he quickly becomes a business man. He quickly becomes a mechanic, a financier, or a salesman. He does not hesitate to identify himself with what he is doing.

With a woman it is quite different. A woman is not easily satisfied, she is very demanding about certain things. She demands that what she is doing reflect herself in some way. She wants to put her mark on the things she is doing, so that her character shines through in some way. This is true whether she is decorating a home or working in an office. She wants to personalize the work and the objects around her. While a man is willing to work in a bare office, a woman wants it to have a certain décor.

At heart a man is made for work. He enjoys conquering and reshaping the material world, for eight hours or so a day, and then he is content. But a woman must spend all her time humanizing the people around her. She is never finished with her work. A man's thoughts are directed towards the external world; he is not so deeply interested in human and personal values. A woman is in closer touch with the pulse of life; she is interested in human beings, particularly her husband and her children.

Now we are at a turning point in history. Men can go into a profession that really interests them, they can enjoy the benefits of leisure, they can develop their human qualities. At the same time, women now have a window on the world; they can engage in activities outside the home. Thus men and women are becoming truly equal. Now, outside the home, women can inject the feminine touch. They can show their interest in people and help them to become truly persons; they can imbue truly human values into the routine of social life, a task which has been neglected by men.

The whole rhythm of our civilization is changing, and parents must realize this. They must teach their sons to attach as much importance to their marriage as to their job. They must teach their daughters the value of an education, so that they will be able to do something else besides being a mother.

Now you may say that a woman should be entirely dedicated to the home; that if she does not create a home, her husband will never do it. That is probably true, but I do not think that contradicts what I have said. The woman must create an atmosphere in the home for her husband and her children, but she must also remain a living person in her own right. She needs some kind of outside work, performed in a feminine way, to develop all of her capabilities.

I remember reading a story once about a woman who was totally dedicated to her husband and her children. She spent her whole effort on them, and they eventually began to look on her as a piece of furniture. When her husband needed advice, she noticed that he went to some other woman and asked her. When her children had to make some decision, they talked it over with their friends. She had forgotten to stay alive as a person, and no one dreamed of treating her as such.

Much of the confusion among our young people today is the fault of their parents. Their parents have not developed and grown as persons. The world and its changing rhythms seem to have passed their parents by, so they cannot come to their parents for advice. Their parents did everything for them and, lacking convictions themselves, they have not been able to teach their children to face up to life. Their parents did everything for them, except help them to build character.

Heine once looked at several imposing cathedrals and said, "How magnificent they are. The people who built these cathedrals had convictions; we only have opinions. But you can't build cathedrals with opinions."

Today's young people were raised by people who never took the time to face life and fashion personal convictions. So they were unable to teach their children how to confront life and hold to one's own conviction.

You must free yourself from this condition if you want to raise your children as human beings. You must react against the intolerable aspects of life and gain mastery over them. You must get rid of the hangover caused by propaganda and hidden persuaders. You must see the raucous cries of the rebellious teenager as a cry of despair, as a plea for values and personal commitment, as a quest for some purposeful outlet.

Today's young people should rebel. They should rebel against the flabby, boneless character of modern civilization. They should learn how to choose on their own, how to affirm their freedom and their manhood, how to read a book critically, how to pass wise judgment on the passing scene. If they had gotten that training from their parents, they would not have to flee to hippie colonies.

CHAPTER 7

Being a Parent

Many men have children.
Few children have fathers.

I want to discuss what it means to be a parent. It seems to me that maternal and paternal love surpasses all other loves in intensity, even conjugal love. In fact conjugal love, at its best and most unselfish, is an echo of parental love.

A real woman is something of a mother to her husband. She sends him back into the world day after day. Now do not get me wrong. I am not in favor of wives who are too maternalistic towards their husbands. A too motherly wife can make an infant out of her husband, for he is inclined in that direction anyway. I think it is a bad sign when a man calls his wife "mama." But the fact is that she does help him to face the world, even as she helps her children.

A mother sends her children out into the world. She restores their self-confidence and helps them to face the unknown. In the same way, she recharges her husband so that he can make a splash in the outside world. Her confidence and her support help him to believe in himself.

And a husband is something of a father to his wife. In his arms she finds new strength and hope and courage. Each helps the other to do what he or she could not do alone.

While a woman tends to be sure of herself most of the time and to take charge of annoying little details, she has moments of abysmal depression and uncertainty. She is a sailboat, moving along briskly in the wind but totally at a loss when the wind dies down. A man has his little outboard motor. He putters along through it all, managing to make some progress in all kinds of weather.

So husband and wife have roles to play vis-à-vis each other. He plays father for her sometimes; she plays mother for him sometimes. And I want you to understand why I consider this paternal and maternal role more exalted than their role as lovers. It is not because conjugal love demands reciprocity, or involves physical union. (Beware of all this talk about "purely spiritual" or "platonic" love.) It is because parental love necessarily involves an unconditional commitment; this commitment should exist in conjugal love, but it can easily fade away.

Where children are involved, one cannot abandon them. One cannot claim the right to give up hope in them, to drop out from fatigue. That is the way it should be with one's spouse, if one really loves that person.

But what does being a parent mean? It is the most profoundly religious experience that a man can have. God is a father. And the only way we can become divine is to become a father or a mother. When someone comes to me in confession, he says, "Bless me, Father, for I have sinned."

In his book on the meaning of monasticism, Louis Bouyer says that the goal of monastic life is spiritual fatherhood. Those who see contemplatives "lost in God" had better take heed. At some point a monk must become a father; otherwise, he has made a mess of his monastic life. Notice that all the great founders of religious orders did become fathers at some point. They ended up by establishing a community. There is no way to approach God really except by becoming a father or a mother.

What does it mean to be a father? What does it mean to be a mother? Let me put it this way. If a person is not a father or a mother, he is a parasite and a miser. He uses things and acquires possessions, but he gives nothing. To be a father or a mother is to be an ingenue, to communicate one's life and joy to others so that they in turn can be fathers and mothers.

You enable your children to become fathers and mothers when their time comes. That is precisely what God did with all of us. He was an ingenue, who created the world so that he could share his life, his generosity, and his joy.

And while I am on this point, let me straighten out St. Ignatius on one item. If you go through the Ignatian exercises, you will find this basic theme headlining the first week: "Man was created to praise and serve God and, in this way, to save his soul." Absolute heresy! A perfect slogan for paganism! God created man to praise and serve him? Can you picture a father who begets children to praise and serve him? What egocentrism! Yet we hear it often: "God created the world to show forth his glory."

What is the glory of God? God takes glory in showing how much he can love. So if we want to express it right, we must say that "God created man so that he could serve and love man, and thus teach man to love and serve his fellow men." God created man to shower his love and his service on this creature. He would love and serve man so much that man, in turn, could become a father to his fellow men.

God did more than give us all he has. He also permitted us to become fathers and mothers. He did not keep us tied to strings on his finger. We have tasted his joy and his life to such an extent that we too want to be God, to be fathers and mothers.

God is in the service of man. He created the world to show the extent of his love. The Incarnation would have taken place no matter what, and the crucifixion is the acme of creation. God wanted to show us how much he can love.

To be a parent is to show how much you can love, how much you can suffer, how much you can create, how much you can serve. Parenthood is obviously as spiritual as it is physical. Everyone is called to become a father or a mother throughout their life, and there are no limits to this spiritual fertility.

Herein lies our most indelible resemblance to God himself. "Evil as you are, you know how to love your children," remarked Christ. That trait of our father cannot be erased, it seems. If you want to prove this to yourself, put it to the test with a problem child. Today, you know, you cannot get far with children by talking to them about God the Father. The father image only provokes resentment and anger in them, because their experience with father has often not been a happy one.

So what do we do with these problem children? The answer is simple: put them in charge of someone weaker and more helpless than themselves. This will draw out the paternal qualities that lie buried in the depths of their being, the qualities that surface when we discover that someone depends on us. It is not so much the example of our own father and mother that teaches us how to be parents; it is this summons put to us by the needs of someone who depends on us.

As you know, Abraham was the first Christian. In the Mass

we invoke "our father, Abraham." Well, when God wanted to show Abraham who God was, what did he do? He did not preach a sermon to him or give him a course in religion. He made Abraham a father, at the age of 99. He taught Abraham existentially, as they say today. And in his experience of fatherhood, Abraham got a complete course in religion. He learned what it means when someone is totally dependent on us, how our heart becomes capable of infinite love in such a situation.

Those who depend on us exercise complete dominion over our heart. We can be very independent towards our superiors and towards those on whom we depend. But we are terribly dependent on those who depend on us. Against them there is no defense, no holding back, no chance for egocentrism. Some cynical people say that this is why women pledge obedience to their husbands.

Do you know the story of St. Theresa and her confessor? Theresa was a vibrant and enthusiastic person, and she thought her confessor was the greatest. She wanted to establish a close relation with him, but he chose to maintain an air of independence towards her. So do you know what she did? She swore obedience to him. That is woman's ace-in-the-hole in dealing with men. What could her confessor do but counsel and advise her? We depend very much on those who depend on us.

So God made Abraham a father. Abraham learned what it means to suffer for someone else, to go through life with an open wound in one's heart which can never be closed. And since God wanted to teach Abraham everything about fatherhood, since he wanted him to glimpse the heart of God, he taught Abraham how to give up his son. Isaac did not die, but Abraham went from death to resurrection. Through the test which God put to him, he learned that he could exercise an even loftier type of paternity. And every parent must learn the same lesson. He must come to realize that his children have a right to gain independence from him, that in this new-found independence they will establish an even better relationship with us. We all must teach our children to move away from us.

The central lesson of Christianity may well be that God depends on us more than we depend on him, that parents depend more on their children than children depend on them. To be a child means to look forward to the day when you will be free of your parents. To be a parent means to remain ever open to your children.

As far as life and grace are concerned, we depend on God of course. But in the order of love God depends on us, because he loves us more than we love him. Look at God on the Cross and tell me who is the more dependent, the more vulnerable, the more powerless: God or us? God, obviously. Now you can begin to appreciate the mystery of fatherhood. Now you can begin to see what Christ meant when he said, "Who sees me, sees the Father."

A father is someone who has torn down his defenses against someone else. That is what God did with us. He said to himself, "I will give them total freedom. But I will love them so much, pardon them so often, and suffer so patiently for them that they will eventually wake up to the love I have for them."

When two people get married, they cannot give each other guarantees that they will always be patient and loving towards each other. Each one can only say to himself, "I will love this person so much and forgive her so often that she (or he) will eventually wake up to the love I have for her." And the same is true with regard to your children. You cannot be assured that they will be bright or clever or respectful. All you can do is love them so much that they will eventually wake up to your love for them. This is the mystery of parenthood and, I think, it is the central mystery of love.

To teach a child religion is to reveal the Father to them. That is the first religious lesson we must get across to them. And, for better or for worse, their idea of God will always be colored to some extent by their picture of you. What you must do is help them to move beyond this picture. You must help them to learn that you can make mistakes, that you can be nervous and unfair, so that they can move beyond you. Their image of you colors their image of God, and this fact is laden with consequences.

For a long time your children thought that you were omnipotent. Your presence could take care of any accident, any sickness, any unhappiness. A child in the hospital does not call for the doctor, he calls for his mommy and daddy. Through their experiences with you, they learn what God's merciful power is.

It is in the home that they also learn what justice is. At school they soon see that the sneak and the apple-polisher can fool teacher. In the playground they soon discover that the bully can rule the roost. At home, however, everyone is given his due and put in his proper place. Mama is not fooled, and justice is meted out impartially. It is in your home that your children first learn about the justice of God.

But love is the chief lesson learned in the home. You tell your children that God is love. But what can they know about God or love if they do not experience these things in the family? How can they know what you mean when you say God is love, if they have not seen you two love each other, if they have not seen you love them. So many children today do not experience this capital lesson in their homes.

What is the ruling force in the world? Is it money, or force, or technology, or propaganda? Or is it love? It is in the home that your children will find an answer to this question, and it is to be hoped, the answer will be love.

Do you remember Christ's remark: "He who lives by the sword will die by the sword"? The remark should not be interpreted as a condemnation of military service. Nor does it justify the conscientious objector outright. I personally think that a man should be free to be a conscientious objector, that it can be a prophetic role; but I do not think it can be shown to be an absolute necessity. The point of Christ's remark is simply that once you get tangled up in violent means, you are caught in a vicious circle. A Christian should find ways to break this vicious circle.

The only life-creating force in the world is love. No matter how powerful other forces may seem to be, they are destructive in the end. Only love can create new beings. Other types of force give rise to reactions, but the great changes in the life of humanity have been wrought by love. It is love that elevates man to a state of new awareness.

Christ said, "Love your enemies. Do good to those who hate you. Pray for those who persecute you. Then you will be like your Father in heaven." What did he mean? He simply meant that we should not be "against" something. We should not get caught up in the vicious circle that enmeshes our enemies. We must be creative and inventive like our Father in heaven. He lets the sun shine on the just and unjust. He lets the rain fall on the just and unjust. If we live by the sword, our future will be boxed in. There are times, perhaps, when we must take up the sword; but the Christian should be inventive enough to find better alternatives.

It is in the bosom of the family that a child experiences love. There he learns how to love; there he learns what happiness it can bring. If he does not learn that lesson in your home, he will be castrated for life.

Fortunately, we all are reborn several times during our life. Around seven, around twelve, and around eighteen, a child begins a new stage in life. However, if he does not discover love at one of these stages, his life will be a barren affair.

If this child is not accepted and loved, he will never be able to accept others or love them. His grasp will become insatiable, because his need for acceptance and love has never been satisfied. The "problem child" is not looking for more love; he is looking for his fair share of love. He will get it one way or another: either you will give him his share, or he will exact it from you by being difficult or sickly. If you do not give it to him, he will pressure you into it somehow.

The big problem in most families is a lack of balance. The mother usually fulfills her role as mother, but the father is just not there. Some men are great fathers, to be sure; they seem to have an instinct for it. But most men go through a long apprenticeship before they become good fathers. And our present-day civilization, the fruit of a long past, makes the father feel that the mother should fulfill this dual role.

Not long ago a teacher friend of mine suggested this composition topic to his teenage students: "What will your future home be like?" They were to describe how they would act when they became fathers and mothers. In their compositions, twenty-seven out of thirty students complained about their fathers. Twenty-seven out of thirty!

The home is a peaceful place until the father gets home. Then terror breaks loose. He tries to compensate for his absence, and he goes to extremes. He is either over-indulgent or overly severe. So the mother must step in to maintain some sort of balance.

But the fact is that children need the father as much as they need the mother. And the daughter will need the father as much as his son will. There are still some fathers around who think only of their sons. They are quick to tell you how many sons they have, but they mutter unintelligibly when you ask them about their daughters. They eventually get over this, but it takes a long time for some.

Fathers should realize that their daughters have a great need of them. It is they who bring their daughters out into the world. At first the daughter feels that every man she loves is already taken: papa has mama, God has the Blessed Virgin. She has no incentive to grow up. You must give her that incentive. The father must make her feel that she can give delight to a man. He must help her to identify with her mother, to make her feel that she can be a mother some day. In like manner, the mother must help her sons to identify with their father; she must help them to feel that they too can delight a woman some day, as daddy delights her. Your son needs you both; your daughter needs you both.

The mother is obviously in a more advantageous position to do all this. She is closer to the children. Her essential role is to serve as a connecting link between the children and their father. But her job is often complicated by the fact that daddy is not there. She needs him to make certain decisions and to collaborate in certain areas, but she is confronted with a vacant chair. And the children, faced with this vacant chair, turn back towards their mother. The son's chances of growing up like a man and the daughter's chances of growing up to be a real woman are impaired by that vacant chair.

There is another problem. A woman generally loves readily and without having to find reasons. She loves her husband because he is her husband; she loves her children because they are hers. A man, however, wants to have reasons. He wants to love his children because they have done something of which he can be proud. But this is putting the cart before the horse. Your child must know he is loved before he can do something to make you proud of him. If you wait for them to earn your love, you will wait forever. In fact, they will give you every reason to support the bad opinion you have of them.

I think every child wants to resemble his or her father or mother; but they will rarely admit this. Generally a boy has lost all hope of becoming like his father, because his father has discouraged him. So he protests that he has no desire to be like his father.

The best thing you can do for your children is let them know that you were no better at their age. Just think back a bit and you will find that this idea is not too far-fetched. Your daughter has an innocent flirtation at fifteen, dangerous only in that she is secretive about it. But she won't talk to her mother about it because she feels her mother won't understand. After all, mama never loved anyone before dad. And where did she get that idea? Obviously, she got it from her parents, who never let her know that they too were young and had problems. If you had told her a little about yourself, then she would say something like this: "Gee, my mother is a fantastic person, but she was no better than me at my age. So I have a great future in front of me. I can become a fantastic person too."

You just cannot imagine how children live up to the opinions you have of them. If you tell your son he is lazy and crazy, he will prove it to you in short order. He will become imprisoned in your judgment, which you take so lightly, and the consequences could be very serious.

The prime quality of an educator is optimism. He has confidence in his pupils. A child has little reason to be confident in himself; it is the most difficult period of life. The only reason he has for self-confidence is the fact that you have confidence in him. If your confidence wavers, he is lost. Your pessimistic forecasts for his future will only confirm his own doubts and misgivings. What you must do is give him unlimited credit.

A person who has developed a personal sense of freedom and real convictions can exercise great authority over others. He gives them security and self-confidence. But "authority" as such has lost its force in our present-day educational system. The social structures of the past are now being challenged and attacked. It is a very serious matter, because your children need your influence, however much they may challenge your authority.

What are we to do? What we must do is win over the internal conviction of our young people. The abstract principle of authority is not enough. Notice how in many areas the signs and tokens of authority are being dropped. The priest is donning a business suit, the nun is altering her habit. Today's people are interested in the person underneath the uniform, not in the uniform itself.

So what are parents to do? You must assert your authority because your children need it, but you must be able to explain and justify your course of action and your decision. You must show them that you are not asking them to obey you, but to obey a higher law which you yourselves obey.

Subjection to another person has always struck me as a degrading thing. Your children should not be subject to you. But you have the right and the obligation to do your duty towards them. And your authority over them is ultimately based on the reasons that justify your course of action. Your children are still weak and will find it difficult to act on the basis of conviction; but they will understand your reasoning, and they will gradually learn from you how to act out of conviction. If you do not teach them this lesson, they will never have the courage to act out of conviction. But you must remember that your authority is in the service of your children.

"Authority," in the bad sense of the word, must never be exercised in the domain of religion. The great advantage of living in a truly Christian family is that the parents' respect for God and the sacred is so great that they do not have to command their children to believe in God or practice their religion. Vatican II upheld the religious freedom of the non-believer. It is high time we respected the conscience of the child!

When a child refuses to pray or go to Mass, there is only one intelligent response: "You are still very young. For the next few months you don't have to go to Mass. But you have to think this question over very seriously. It is a very important matter, and you must think about it as an adult would." The very fact that your child has already made this decision, however, suggests that you have missed the boat in some way. You may have abused your authority, or rushed things along a bit too fast.

As I said before, every child wants to be like his parents. If religion is an adult affair in your house, he will want to take part in it. If it is a child's affair, he will be anxious to outgrow it as you were.

Nothing could be worse than forcing children to pray, to go to Mass, or to go to confession. And yet it has been done for centuries. Look at how Christ operated in the Gospels. He never forced his disciples to pray. In fact, it seems he never even suggested it to them. But he prayed himself. He went off by himself and spent whole nights in prayer. When he returned to them, he must have radiated something special: a calm, an assurance, a peacefulness that struck them. They must have wondered what it would be like, if they could pray like that. Then one day they approached him: "Lord, teach us to pray."

If you teach religion, your first job is to get your pupils to make such appeals to you. All your teaching is in vain, if you cannot get them to do that. If they have no desire to become like you, there is no sense trying to give them some other model to imitate. If you know how to pray, they will want to pray too. If you have become someone worth imitating, they will approach you. You can be sure of that.

Ordinarily, however, we reverse the whole process. For fourteen years or so, we force the catechism and the sacraments upon them, somehow sensing that they would never accept these things on their own. Then, just when they are capable of revolting against this regime, as they usually do, we pat ourselves on the back and say: "Well, we have done our duty." Indeed!

What does the Church really ask of parents? She asks that by the time your children are eighteen, you will have given them some understanding of God, some taste for prayer, some appreciation for the Mass. Take it slow, there is plenty of time. This is a slow training program for the heart, not a quickie course at summer school. And pay more attention to yourself than to your children. Do your children seem anxious to join you in prayer? If not, it is probably you who are at fault, not they. What does the Mass mean to you? Where should you change?

We should not ask children to memorize answers before

111

they have realized what the questions are. They should eventually come to regard prayer as such an adult thing that they are anxious to take part in it.

A child has an almost insatiable capacity to assimilate religious values. He will outstrip you in short order, unless you dishearten him by abusing your authority. And if you do, he will have his revenge. How often children fool around during family prayer: you have pressured them into it, so they retaliate with their own brand of pressure. Whenever an educator tries to use pressure on his students, they will resist somehow. An undercurrent of discontent and opposition runs through every classroom, according to one educator.

So you say to me, "What are we to do? Let them have their way?" Well, in every domain besides religion, you should exercise your authority, giving reasons for your decisions. You must do this for their own good, but just make sure that they know they are submitting to some higher principle, not to your private whim. But the realm of religion is so sacred that it must involve interior consent; you cannot exercise authority here.

I should like to see much more vitality and enthusiasm in the realm of moral education. You do not have to debate the supper hour, or bedtime, or homework with your children; there are plenty of areas where you can assert your rightful authority. But there should be complete freedom in the domain of religion, and a real attempt to awaken enthusiasm and interest.

It is in the realm of religion that your role as mother and father finds fullest expression. And the most important lesson in religion that you can give your children is this: in the realm of religion, we spend our whole life learning. In this area, you are merely the elder brothers and sisters of your children. In this realm, you too are still sons and daughters. In this realm you too have much to learn, even from them, and you can exchange ideas with them.

I have heard many parents say that they have never been able to get their children to talk to them. I have also heard the same complaint from many children. Which reminds me of an incident that is worth recalling here. The son of one of my friends had done badly at school, and his father decided to punish him by keeping him at home while the rest of the family went to the seashore. About two weeks later, I met his son and asked him how he was enjoying his vacation. "It's the best vacation I've ever had!" he said. "How is that?" I asked, somewhat perplexed. "Well, I see my father every day. He takes me to his office sometimes. I watch him work, and sometimes he lets me help him. The other day he took me to a restaurant, and we talked and talked. I have never been so happy." And his father thought he was punishing him!

Yes, many parents complain that their children do not confide in them. But there is only one way to win the confidence of your children, and this is to confide in them. If you never talk about yourself, why should your children bother to talk about themselves? If you talk to your children, if you confide in them, if you listen to them, they will feel that their advice is important and they will confide in you in turn. But if you stop talking to them, they will eventually have nothing to say to you. They will have learned their lesson—from you.

It is in the realm of religion above all that there can be a communion between parents and their children. But you must stay young and childlike enough to trade confidences with them, to discover things together, to share your experiences.

113

CHAPTER 8

The Universal Dimensions of Love

All love, particularly the tested love of marriage and parenthood, has a universal dimension. For every real love is a taste of the love of God himself. Since it is the only thing worth making eternal, it is the experience in which we truly find ourselves.

Marriage exacts a demanding fidelity from us. It asks us to be faithful to a person who will turn out to be quite different from the person to whom we pledged fidelity at the start. Indeed, it will ask us to help him become this different person.

Parenthood is even more exacting. For the love we have for our own children is, in the last analysis, the love we would have had for any child.

Undoubtedly, no one else could have tapped these wellsprings of love within us so well as our spouse. But once this love has been tapped, once it has grown and developed, it is so comprehensive that it has actually taken on universal dimensions.

The decisive indication of a couple's maturity is their new-found vulnerability. They have taken down their defenses. They are open to each other. They summon up the best from each other and quietly dampen each other's baser drives.

This universal dimension, which your love takes on in marriage, is the natural development of your love. Nothing is more consoling and salutary than a home filled with this kind of love.

If Christianity has lost its power to attract people, it is because there is no longer an environment of love to be found. This environment of love, the Church, is mirrored in that microcosm of love, the family. Few families radiate love, few groups have the power to attract people into them. The Holy Spirit, the Spirit of love, is no longer visible in the world; and the only way to win over the world is to make this Spirit visible.

Our civilization is terribly in need of unity, yet it seems almost totally incapable of achieving it. We are all tied to each other in many ways, but there is no love visible in our interdependence. Our collectivist structures grind down the individual because they operate in an inhuman way. We live in a dustbowl of isolated individuals. These dried bones must be suffused with a breath of new life, with the spirit of faith and love.

Nothing is more plain to see than the spirit of love, and nothing is more convincing. Those fortunate enough to encounter and live this spirit can never doubt its existence again. If families could get together and radiate their own happiness and generosity, their impact on the world would be enormous. They would exercise a great and important apostolate.

That is why I stressed the importance of devoting the first years of your marriage to creating this atmosphere of conjugal union. Even children take a back seat to this task of creating an atmosphere of mutual collaboration. How much study and training have you put into your professional life? How much have you put into your marriage training?

Without this spirit of unity, the couple's apostolate would be greatly diminished. Without this spirit of unity, they would not be able to radiate love to others. Without this spirit of unity, they would be play-acting rather than fulfilling their mission.

In marriage the influence of the couple should shine through to others. Each should radiate the new-found brilliance of their union. Each should add luster to the radiance of the other. You would do well to check up on yourself, to see if that is true in your case.

Besides creating unity in their marriage and their family life, a couple must radiate this unity in their societal life. They need social relationships, and society needs their joint activity; but the activity of each may differ greatly, of course.

This social dimension is lacking in many homes. The couple's love is an indoor reality which does not get out into the open air. Without a breath of fresh air, it soon becomes stale. The couple has built a fine home, but they have forgotten to leave room for a chimney.

When I preach to young marrieds, I can almost feel the glow of their love for each other. But eventually they settle down in their nest and forget the outside world. And their children do not fail to notice this. Parents must stay in contact with the world, they must have social relationships, if they really want to educate their children for life.

Are you giving or are you going to give your children a real, concrete education—or an abstract one? A concrete education takes in the whole realm of reality and develops all of one's relations with the world. A child must become progressively more aware of his relationships with the outside world. Without these relationships, he cannot develop.

A new-born baby, you see, is an abstraction. By that I mean he lives in isolation. He is not aware of his relations with other human beings. Gradually he enters into relationships with others; with his father and mother, first of all. Then he goes to school and really begins to take part in the world. He plays with his friends, he goes to the store, he joins clubs. He becomes aware of his country, of other countries, of the whole universe. And at the pinnacle of this concrete education stands religion, which deals with the totality of our relationships. Nothing is, or should be, more concrete than religion.

Real education, as I see it, is a vivid awareness of the concrete —a realization that thought and action cannot be separated into isolated compartments. Well, religion is a drive towards totality. Christ is the fullness, the totality, of relationships. That is why every truly concrete thought is religious in nature. Religion should make us realize that our relationships extend to the whole world and to God himself. Sad to say, religion is dying today because it has been turned into an abstraction. The practice of religion has been separated from real life.

The Christian goes to church on Sunday, but the world is the same on Monday. No change has been wrought in the social, political, and economic world. We still are faced with the bomb, with social injustice, and with underdeveloped nations. There is no connection between the Gospel and everyday life, even though Christ said, "By their fruits you will know them."

Whom did Christ bless? Good mothers and fathers? Those who had gotten a good "Catholic" education? No: "Blessed are they who hear the word of God and *put it into practice.*" Christ was a realist.

To educate your children is to teach them about all the relationships they have. Your children will be grown up only when they have been brought into relationship with the whole world, only when they are truly catholic.

When you sit down at a family meal, the whole world is on your table; your food comes from every part of the world. But

117

is the whole world in your mind and your heart and your table talk? Do you try to awaken your children's interest in the world, to get them thinking about its problems?

Every genuine prayer and every loving thought leads to action. It unites us with God, and with the whole world. A truly Christian education enables our children to experience and take part in this dimension of universality. But relatively few Christian children get such an education.

The major problem facing young people is that they do not have a goal, an ideal into which to channel their energies. They have no confidence that they can make an impression on the world, or change it. The world is changing rapidly but their parents, who were involved in this transformation, refuse to shoulder responsibility for it; so they cannot learn responsibility towards the world from their parents.

The delinquent and the hippie have something burning inside their heart. Once upon a time these people were sent out to conquer the world or to win a empire. Today they must find some project worthy of their dedication, or they will revolt against society. And the sad thing is that although many of them have had a "Christian education," they have never enjoyed the concrete experience of real Christian living.

I remember giving a retreat to teaching nuns not too long ago. Near the end of the retreat, one of the nuns had this to say: "Father, in three days you have demolished the religion I have been teaching to students for twenty years; but I think you are quite right. But now what am I to teach them, what am I to say in next year's religion course?" A fair question, but the answer is simple enough: "Lucky you, you don't have to *say* anything about religion any more. Your days of lecturing about religion are over. And your pupils will be delighted. They are sick of hearing about religion. Now you are going to help your pupils to fashion a Christian environment out of their classroom. Make a community out of your classroom. Make it a concrete experience from nine to three every school day. Let your pupils share their experiences, let the most backward students feel free to talk without fear of ridicule, let them trade books and records, let them write little notes to the absentees. In short, let each student feel that he belongs to a community. Then, at the end of the year, read a passage from the Gospel that explains what you have been doing all year."

Present religion courses are a flood of words. We must stop talking about religion and start living it. We have prevented children from ever having faith by stuffing them with sacraments, prayers, and abstract ideas. What have we taught them about living religion? We have reared them in the most egotistical and most pagan style of life imaginable, a style of life which certainly has no need for supernatural supports.

Having nothing to do is what stunts the life of a child. So many parents tell their children to "take it easy" or to "be still." All the effort they have expended in building a home dispenses the child from making any effort at all; they put so much effort into fashioning a home, and their children slowly die in that home because there is nothing for them to contribute to it. Parents have the right to rest from their labors in the home that they have built; but they should not let the home become their children's coffin.

Today's parents must be active in the world, for their children's sake. The children deserve to have their parents' full-time attention when they are very young, of course, but gradually the parents should introduce the children to their apostolate. Once upon a time parents used to sneak out of the house in the evening, so the children would not see them going. Today parents should do it openly, and share their experiences with their children. The children will catch on quickly enough, and it will be a big step forward.

While I am on the subject of the apostolate, let me say that egotism can dominate one's apostolate and one's work very easily. I am suspicious of the person who feels "called" to some peculiar task of his own. Those who are engaged in an apostolate should look into their motives constantly, to see whether they are selfish or not.

Always be a little suspicious of yourself. Make sure you know the real reasons behind what you are doing. It often seems easier to be successful outside than to be successful with yourself; to make a hit with someone else's wife rather than with your own; to bring up someone else's kids rather than your own. The other person's backyard often does look greener. We must frankly recognize this temptation, and then do our best to overcome it.

That is why we must keep an eye on ourselves. We must make sure that we are not trying to serve ourselves in serving others. Delve into yourself once in awhile. Read a book that makes you do some thinking. Try a little prayer. Talk to your wife and your children. Ask yourself, "Who is this person that I am?"

A crass spirit concentrates solely on what it possesses or what it does. A noble spirit concentrates on what it is. We must keep our own spirit groomed, and this requires some attention and care. Spiritual books suggest a regular routine of such care, but I do not think that that is the proper approach. Individuals vary, so each person must groom himself accordingly. When you need to stop and think things over, do it; how often you do this is for you to decide.

Some of the questions you might ask yourself: "Does my spouse share in my life? Has my work been transformed by my marriage? Do our children share in our life and activity?"

Every human life should have both a horizontal and a vertical thrust. Horizontally, it should take part in the progress of the human race and the development of the temporal world. It should take cognizance of the fact that God's salvation plan is meant to transform the world. Our actions should have ties with the actions of others which precede and follow ours. At the same time, our actions should have an intrinsic value of their own. They should relate vertically to God, so that our every action would be worth making eternal if we should die on the spot.

The strict contemplative, for example, fulfills only the vertical dimension. His every action bespeaks what he wants to do for all eternity, but it does not relate to the human world. His actions do not tell us that a Christian is primarily someone who loves and seeks to save the world. By the same token, the activist who does not develop his interior life fails to develop the vertical dimension; he fails to appreciate the eternal value of any and every act he performs. None of us is truly adult unless we develop both dimensions. And it is in prayer that we take cognizance of all our relationships and of these two important dimensions.

Religion comes from the Latin word *re-ligare,* which means "to tie together again." That is what we must do: tie the strands of our life together. If we do not do this, then we rush pell-mell into one activity after another; we do not know where we are going or what the value of it all is.

Everyone talks about the "progress" of the world. But how do you know it is progress, if you have no scale of values and no worthwhile goal in mind? If it is an undefined progress, how do you know it is progress? What value is there in each act of yours? Is each act worth making eternal? And what value is there in the whole scheme of your activity?

If you dream of only the future having value, then you do not believe in any values at all. To say that we shall survive in the happiness of a generation yet unborn is to say that we shall survive solely as vegetables or minerals. If such a survival is to be human, it must involve self-awareness because that is the chief characteristic of a human being.

You must have something worth living for right now. You must have something worth dying for right now. If you do not have it now, you will never have it. If your actions do not have value right now, then they are not worth anything. This is the element of personal and transcendent value which Christianity can contribute to the world. Many political slogans are noble and religious, but they lack this element of personalism and transcendence. "If one man is enslaved, I am not free." What a noble and religious sentiment! But what does it mean, if it is not grounded on a system of personal and transcendent values? That is the question which we must put to the modern world.

CHAPTER 9

Before Marriage

Marriage is undergoing great transformations at the present time. Unfortunately, men's ideas and attitudes sometimes do not change as rapidly as institutions. Notice how some people have reacted unfavorably to the unspectacular innovations of Vatican II. The greatest danger facing you who are not yet married is that you will get married with the ideas and attitudes of your parents, even though your marriage will not have the same meaning, the same purpose, and the same supports that theirs did.

Let me single out three stages in the evolution of marriage, so that you can see what I am talking about.

Stage 1. For centuries, up to about 1918, marriage was primarily an "institution." Since it involved social and economic status, parents had a dominant role to play in the question of marriage. It was a question of eking out a living, of surviving in a world of poverty. The death-rate was so high that economic necessity ruled everything. In thinking about marriage, a person had to be reasonable. Love had to be sacrificed to duty. The "rebels," those who married for love, became the heroes and heroines of romantic literature.

Stage 2. It is only recently that the upward curve of industrialization freed marriage from harsh economic constraints. But young people were not prepared for this sudden change. Your parents got married in this confusing period of transition. Marriage as an institution had lost the solidity and stability it once had. But people got married with the old idea that the institution, backed up by the Church and the state, could protect them from their own weaknesses; that the Church and the state could give marriage a value that they themselves could not. They were free to marry the person of their choice, but they were given no real preparation for this new state of affairs. How could they be taught by an older generation who had been reared with the notion of "duty"?

Stage 3. Now it is your turn. And the danger confronting you is that you may not realize that you yourselves have to make something out of your marriage. You may unwittingly get married for the same reasons your parents did, even though your world is different.

Many of you will say that there is no danger on that score. You will assure me that your ideas are completely different from those of your parents. But, alas, people do not get married on ideas and they do not live on ideas. I know many young people who got married for the best of reasons, not realizing that they were really motivated by the taboos and prejudices that had been imbedded in their unconscious. They had actually been guided by their super-ego.

All of this would be fine, if it were the same world as that of their parents. But it is not, and this could lead to disaster. The extrinsic reasons which once precipitated marriages—economic, social, religious, and so on—will no longer do. No longer can a woman dedicate herself as a willing slave to her husband. No longer can a man expect his wife to be a devoted chattel. The modern woman will not accept the marriage mythology that is still propagated in some marriage manuals. Even Jean Guitton is still saying things like this: "Woman cannot be the priest, but she can be the victim." If a man gets married with those ideas in his head, he will be in for a rude shock. His wife will not accept the prison of marriage for long. She will want to remain alive and vibrant.

In short, there is only one solid basis for marriage today: a real and vibrant love. None of the old reasons will do. You just cannot get married to preserve the family honor, to maintain the family tradition, or simply to have children. As I have already pointed out, you must have better reasons for living and better reasons for marrying.

What does this mean? It means that we must develop a whole educative process concerning love. Let me try to trace the outlines of such a process.

Time to Know Each Other

You must really know each other before you get married. It seems to me that three years would represent the minimum amount of time required. So courtship would involve at least three years.

Now I know very well that the old-time educators counselled against over-long engagements. But look how it was in those days. People often got engaged without ever seeing each other; they had to be engaged before they could even go together. And when they were together, there was always a chaperone between them.

I am for long courtships because I am for a marriage choice that is truly free. There should be several years of seeing each other, of taking trips together, of working together in small ways. The couple should have opportunities to see each other as they really are, to have arguments and reconciliations, to suffer the pangs of temporary separation. In this way they can gradually learn how important it is for them to be together, while preserving their right to break up if this seems the right thing to do.

This is one reason why I advise against pre-marital relations. I shall discuss this further later on. But let me say right here that intercourse may dull their attention to other important aspects of their relationship. It may cloud their judgment on the most important question, which has not yet been resolved.

Many young people will object that three years is too long a time. But stop and think for a minute. How long does it take you to get an education? How long does it take you to train for a career? Look at all the exams you have to pass, all the class-time you have to put in. And is not your marriage as important?

Men, unfortunately, think they are always ready for love. They think they are born "pros" in this field when, in fact, they have much to learn.

Moreover, maturity is a longer and slower process today. The human animal, of its very nature, has a long childhood; it is one of the things which allows man to develop his complex potential. The chicken can peck right about three hours after birth; we are a bit slower about growing up. Are you the same person you were last year? What will you be like next year? Think about it.

Only long experience can help you to decide about marriage. Time is the great testing ground for love. It is only gradually that a man realizes that he needs this woman to become truly himself, that she will be able to inject new life into him when he is down, and that he in turn will be able to make her a real

woman. It is only slowly that people learn that the love of another must be the foundation of their life.

Rilke was once asked by a young man whether the latter
should become a poet. His answer was simple: "You should
know that yourself. If you'd rather die than not write poetry,
then you are a poet." And so it should be with love. If you
cannot live without that girl or guy, then you had better marry
that person.

A Few Questions to Ask Yourself

You can check up on yourself to some extent by asking yourself
some questions. It is very important to do so, because we can
delude ourselves very easily in this area. Everyone thinks he or
she is ready for love when he gets married, but it soon becomes
evident how many were not prepared for the step. So let us do
some checking up.

First, we can consider some positive signs:

(1) Never marry someone who expects a total change in his
life after marriage. Never marry someone who was never happy
until he met you. If your would-be spouse expects all his happiness to come from you, you may soon fail him; and he will be
as miserable as before. The person you marry should have found
some happiness on his own. To be sure, a person may well have
had a long and unhappy childhood; but the point is that he or
she should be able to make some changes in it before he gets
married to you. If he has not made this effort before, he
may not make it after his marriage either.

Do not marry someone who was not able to love the people
he lived with before he met you. You will be living with this

person a long time, and it is a bad sign if he or she has never been able to love anyone before.

The same goes for yourself. Do not look for happiness only after you are married. Your chances of having a happy marriage are much greater if you have been able to fashion a happy life before marriage.

In this respect, our age offers great advantages to girls. They can go to college and post-graduate school. They can assert their independence and pursue a career. The single girl is no longer an object of scorn; in fact, she is often more of a person than those of her classmates who marry before her. It is to be hoped that she will benefit from her experience to become a better person, to contribute more to the marriage she ultimately enters.

(2) In my young days, fellows were told to observe the mother of the girl they love. The half-truth in this piece of advice was that daughter would be like mother in another twenty years. I would not take this idea too seriously, but I would suggest that you observe your loved one with others. How does she act in her home, among your friends, with other people in general? She will probably act much the same with you some day.

(3) Do not marry a deadbeat, who is looking forward to marriage in order to have something to do. Seek out a mate who is vibrant and alive and interested in many things now. If he or she is not bored now, the chances are that he will not get bored with you when you are married.

The Hidden Persuaders

When someone you know tells you that he is going to introduce you to a friend of his, you can form some idea of his friend.

128

When this same person tells you that he is going to introduce you to his wife, you had better be prepared for surprises.

The people you went to school with were intelligent in your eyes, I am sure. Yet when you meet them twenty years later and see whom they married, you are filled with wonder. How in heaven's name did he ever pick her?

The fact is that despite all appearances and all the good reasons people can muster, it is almost always instinct that prevails in this area. Our need and our appetite for love is very great, and it can distort our picture of reality very quickly. It is this appetite which makes the menu look better than it is, which drives us into the arms of the first person who comes along. We find the reasons afterward.

Instinct operates automatically. Indeed, if we had been allowed to, we probably would have married a cousin long ago. The seductive web is woven easily, and always with the same lines: "You're the first person who has ever understood me. With you, I can breathe for the first time in my life."

The problem is that authentic love says the same things. The difference is that in true love it is a real discovery. The person really thought he was happy and content until he met this special person. So you see how much care and caution is required.

Physical contact alone is enough to start the whole mechanism in motion. Our emotions come tumbling out, and we have soon said a lot more than we really meant to say.

So what are we to do? How are we to escape the chains of this overweening drive? The answer is that we must put a little effort into our life. It is not as hard as it sounds.

Pascal once said, "We are so proud that we want to conquer the world, but we are so vain that the praise of a few friends satisfies us." Well, our passion for love seems to be insatiable;

but a few good friends, some useful occupations, and an outlet for our zeal will keep our affective life in balance pretty well—while we wait for true love to come along.

It is often the class dunce who gets married first. This person has no other real interest in life, no other outlet for his or her energies. And you do not need a passing grade or a diploma to get married. For many people, love is a passive thing; it allows us to stop fashioning a real life for ourself. But that is not what real love is. Real love summons up all our energies to tackle the new life we have found for ourself.

Do you know the story of the hermit and the young man? It seems there was this young man who was obsessed with thoughts of the opposite sex. He had had a good Christian education, so he never acted on his impulses; but he thought about them all the time. He read the slick girlie magazines, he looked at art books, he consulted dictionaries. But every time he met a girl, he became speechless, even though he was going wild inside. Confession was no help to him, because all the priest could say was, "Pray to the Blessed Virgin, shun the demon of impurity, preserve your virtue, think of your good mother, work at your studies, etc." He was in torment.

Finally, he sought out an old and pious hermit whose wisdom and sanctity were legendary. He explained his plight and the old man listened sympathetically. After listening to him, the hermit simply asked him one question: "The thing that puzzles me is that every girl does this to you. Why is it that there isn't one particular girl that drives you wild? It seems to me that one should be enough for any man." Jolted by this realistic question, the boy replied that he was so disturbed that he could not really distinguish one girl from another.

"Well," said the hermit, "this is what you do. The next time you meet a girl, take a close look at her. Try to determine if you really like the impression she makes on you. I guarantee that you will not find many who measure up to your standards."

Diffidently, the boy decided to follow the hermit's advice. The next time he ran into a girl he overcame his initial confusion and really gave her a good look. To his surprise, a feeling of calm came over him. Emboldened by this experience, he began to be more discerning in his contacts with girls. Upon the advice of the hermit, he began to look for certain qualities in the girls he met: a lively expression, a sympathetic attitude, a certain charm and air of goodness, a love of children, an amiable way with the people around them. And, to make a long story short, he found only one girl that had all these qualities in his eyes. One day he came back to the hermit—a married man.

It is never too early to begin preparing for marriage, even though we should be mature before we do get married. The fellow who never thinks about girls will fall prey to the first one who comes his way. You must fashion your ideal woman and look diligently for her. Only in this way will you manage to escape a wrong choice.

Sex Relations Before Marriage

After all that I have said about the need for long courtship, for sharing experiences together, you are probably wondering whether I am willing to pursue this logic to the bitter end. If two people are going to investigate their relationship in depth, should they not investigate it all the way?

I will try to give you an honest answer, an answer that sheds light on the courtship experience rather than reinforcing the moral and social taboos of the past.

To begin with, we can deplore the mentality that has prevailed up to the present, the code which was imposed on every young girl as the ideal to be sought after: to stay a virgin until the day of the wedding. To the disgust of most young women, their parents seemed only concerned about keeping the betrothed out of bed before the wedding. We shall never know how many couples defied this injunction out of pure spite. To watch his daughter coming down the aisle "intact," totally unprepared for marriage but intact, was the dream of every parent.

In the modern courtship which I have described here, a lengthy process where free choice prevails, one can readily envision the possibility that something might just "happen." And this would not be a castastrophe, if it happened in the course of a serious, well-intentioned attempt by two people to get to know each other.

Before we go any further, let me point out that nothing is more dangerous than an "idealist" marriage. Never marry someone for whom you do not feel a real sexual attraction. The sexual attraction should not be the decisive factor, but it is indispensable. And this attraction will be irresistible only if an engaged couple has not found that true love which injects deep emotion into everything they do together. Sexual attraction is a fine servant but a bad master. It will add spirit and excitement to everything you do together. But if it rules your relationships, then that is a sign of your lack of imagination, of your ennui. If that is all you can ever fall back on, things are in bad shape.

To be sure, you should feel this attraction at work. But you do not necessarily have to pursue it to its ultimate consequences to know that it is at work. Engaged people certainly have the right to display their affection for each other in progressively greater degrees; just make sure that it springs from love and is a manifestation of love, not something else masquerading as love.

You cannot measure these things with a stop-watch or a tape measure. But, as a general principle, I would say that haste in this area is a sign of gluttony and boredom. The tourist who rushes through a sight-seeing trip cannot really be enjoying the passing scenery. True lovers can drink in the delight of being close to each other, of looking into each other's eyes, of holding each other's hand. Every gesture, every touch, has rich meaning for those who truly love.

I would certainly agree that one should never marry someone just to get to bed with that person. And I would certainly say that more than one marriage has come about for that reason. Nothing could be worse than that. If that is the only motive behind it, better by far to go to bed without getting married than to get married to go to bed.

However, a solid education in love and its workings can do a great deal to preclude these dangerous obsessions. Coeducation in large doses, a sound sex education, even trips to respectable nudist camps and psychotherapy may be advisable. The only reservation I have about psychotherapy is that too many therapists recommend going to bed with anyone you can lay your hands on. Those who try this remedy are often worse off than they were at the start.

Now let me explain why I advise against pre-marital intercourse as a general rule. As I see it, the essence of sexual morality is this: the acts have meaning. And the sexual act is an act of total commitment. You can lie with words, but can you lie with your actions? Sexual union is the gift of oneself to another, the total gift of oneself. Can you really make this gesture one moment and then draw back into your own shell the next? If you are not really tied to this other person, what meaning does your act have? It seems to me that you are emptying the gesture of any real meaning. If it is simply a gesture of sympathy or attraction, then what is to stop you from extending it to others after you are married?

I remember preaching a retreat to engaged couples once. During the retreat they kept coming to me in confession with the same opening line: "Father, I committed impure acts with my fiancé." Something had to be done, so I decided to say something about it to them. "My dear young people," I said, "I am shocked by the religious conceptions you entertain. You people love each other. You are going to marry each other. You are already engaged. I am sure that the gestures of affection which you show towards one another are sincere gestures of love. As such, they are essentially good and quite beautiful. Yet you come to me and call them acts of *impurity*. In a few months you will be doing the same things in marriage. And I for one don't see how the Church or anyone else can suddenly transform these *impure* acts into pure ones.

"The basic difference is this. Right now you young men have not made this girl your own. She does not belong to you yet. You aren't feeding her, or clothing her, or building a house around her. You are still free to leave each other, and yet you are acting as if you already belonged to each other. You are doing the wrong thing in trying to get this girl to give herself to someone to whom she does not yet belong. And you may teach her so well that she will not hesitate to do it again some day in the future.

"You, young lady, have not yet made this young man your own. You are not cooking his meals, putting up with his bad temper, or looking at him holding a newspaper between you at the breakfast table. You are treading a dangerous route. Because if you accustom him to having a woman who does not really belong to him, he may never break the habit.

"What I'm saying is that you both must respect the reality of your present situation. You should not play married until you are married."

Well, that started a good discussion. They were not going to let me get away so easily.

"But after all, Father, we want to marry each other. We are pledged to each other with all our heart. Why can't we demonstrate this by our actions?"

"Fine," I said, "you want to get married? Okay, come on into the chapel with me and I'll marry you right away. We'll celebrate your wedding tonight!"

"Now wait a minute, Father. We can't get married right now. Our parents haven't given their consent."

"What in heaven's name does your parents' consent have to do with it, at your age? You obviously want to marry each other. If you are so concerned about your parents' consent, it is probably because you yourselves see some sound sense in the idea of waiting a bit. So it is your idea as well. And if it makes sense to hold off the marriage for a while, doesn't it make equally good sense to hold off the marital activity for a while?"

"Well," said another, "I'd marry her this minute. But I've got to go in the army."

"Why should that hold up your marriage? If you want to belong to each other right away, why not get married right away?"

"Well, we have to look for a house first."

"I don't see why that should hold you up, if you are so anxious to get married. You say it is not the right moment to get married, but you still feel it is the right moment to shack up together. Well, it seems to me that a house is even more necessary for shacking up than for getting married. Or are you planning to shack up in the park?"

You see, there is just the slightest trace of self-deception in their arguments. They have all sorts of good reasons for holding off their marriage. But all these reasons are promptly forgotten when it comes to displaying their love for each other. Why this clandestine love-making? Is it good for their relationship to be teaching each other to be secretive, to have an air of shame surround their actions?

It would certainly be a bad sign if engaged people were not anxious to display their love ever more fully. But, as I see it, it is also a bad sign if such displays become *indispensable*. True love finds joy in being together, in speaking to each other, in doing things together; in this way, it helps to ease the obsessive desire to go to bed together.

If a couple are in such haste to get under the covers, if they have already exhausted their inventiveness, if they are already trying to peek at the last chapter of their novel, I wonder if they will ever really enjoy the fullness of their romance.

The man, in particular, is so quick to be distracted by other things. He so quickly rests on his laurels. If he can make his sexual conquest too easily, there is danger that he will stop working at his marriage very shortly. Marriage is a long proving ground for love, as we have tried to show. If he gets things without much effort, the man may stop making this effort after the first night.

But this same man may be led by the right woman to heights of gentleness and devotion of which he never dreamed himself capable. She may teach him a better love than the one he pictured at the start.

When I speak of the need for long courtships, this does not mean that the couple should assume the conclusion before the courtship is over. It means that they must retain their freedom, ready to back out if it seems to be a mistake, or if someone more suitable comes along. The thing which must be preserved is the freedom of each, and that is what must be respected as well.

Love is so vast, so creative, so full of wonder that it will take us a whole lifetime to learn how to love.

Procreation and Birth Control

I want to say a few words about the problem of birth control, because it would be less than honest to skip over it.

To understand the present situation on this question, we must go far back into Church history. An aura of pagan asceticism has pervaded the Church for many centuries.

What is a pagan? A pagan is someone who tries to gain control over God, to merit God's favor by all sorts of rites and practices. In the primitive Church, for example, there was only one fast day a year, a gesture of amicability towards the Jews who took these things very seriously. Gradually, however, a trend towards asceticism developed in the Church, partially influenced by Judaic tradition.

We find virgins, holy widows who do not remarry, and "chaste" people. But there was much vagueness in these terms. Who is chaste? The person who chooses not to use sex, or the person who keeps control over sex even though he does use it? Does virtue reside in non-use or in proper use, in abstention or in harmonious, integrated utilization? That, you see, is the important question.

Up to now, we can say that the Church's code regarding sexual behavior has been dominated by an air of prohibition. All sorts of sanctions were introduced to get married people to dampen their sex drives. And the prime sanction was the child. If you wanted to play, you would have to pay. The child was the price you paid for your pleasure. St. Augustine and St. Thomas Aquinas had much to do with the formulation of the Church's doctrine on this question. And as far as they were concerned, sexual intercourse always involved at least a venial sin. To atone for this sin, the couple would have to accept the demands of procreation. It was procreation that justified sexual intercourse.

One might say that St. Augustine was hardly in a position to develop a sound doctrine of sexuality. St. Thomas was an ascetic monk, but he relied heavily on St. Augustine in this area because of the latter's experience. St. Thomas regarded Abraham as the model for all Christians; unfortunately, Abraham was a polygamist. You should see the virtuosity he displays in trying to get around that fact!

Today sexuality has been re-examined and given new value. People are trying to make sure that it is an expression of authentic love, and they are less concerned about imposing restrictions.

We can pose the question in several different forms. Should a couple have intercourse because it is the right moment physiologically, or should they have intercourse because they truly love each other—whether the moment is right or not? Should people avoid having intercourse because it is not the right physiological moment, or because their love is not properly disposed at the moment? Which is sacred: biology or love itself?

There are three differing schools of thought in the Church. The first school of thought holds on obstinately to traditional views, as elaborated by Pius XII in particular. Only "natural" methods are justifiable. The thermometer is the guide.

More modern theologians oppose this approach, and they divide up into two schools. The first school says: "Of course, we must respect nature; but we have a right to improve and regulate nature as well. For example, we have a right to intervene to regulate the menstrual cycle. We have a right to keep the woman sterile during the period of lactation, using the pill if necessary." This idea can be carried pretty far, because in some primitive populations where there are few milk cows, the lactation period can go on for two or three years! Moreover, fear of pregnancy can be so severe that it becomes a real neurosis, so medication might well be prescribed.

Interestingly enough, the widest breach in the traditional doctrine of natural methods was introduced by the whole question of rape. That alone might make you wonder a bit! Theologians have long admitted that a raped woman could try to prevent conception in the hours immediately following the rape. Some even went so far as to say that a woman could take contraceptive precautions if she was in danger of being raped. This idea was carried further: if a husband indicated that he was going to keep going, that was moral pressure equivalent to the physical force of rape. Finally, in a period when a woman was in danger of being raped, temporary sterilization might be permitted.

Some of these theologians go even further. Father Joseph Fuchs teaches at the Gregorian University in Rome. He has written that temporary retardation of ovulation, that is, for a few days, can be justified to avoid a particularly vexing menstruation. A woman might be taking a short trip, or attending an important ceremony. That is actually the teaching of the Church at the present time, but few people know it. Certain secrets are guarded zealously, you see. You can whisper it in privileged circles but, for heaven's sake, don't tell the laity about it.

The third school of thought pushes on from there. It says, "If you have gone that far, then we must give up this whole idea of respecting or regulating nature. We must jump to a higher scale of values entirely. Human dignity must be the measuring rod."

Father Eduard Schillebeeckx, the noted theologian to the Dutch hierarchy, put it this way. If you allow the principle of contraception in the case of rape, out of respect for the principle of human dignity, then the law of following nature is not absolute nor morally binding as such. Biological structures as such do not establish a moral obligation; it is human dignity that establishes the obligation, and everything must be subordinated to the principle of human dignity.

Do you have the right to impose children on people who do not want them? Are not the rights of the spouses violated when their marital relations are governed by questions of nature, the thermometer, and the calendar?

So these theologians formulate this position. Man is not obliged to follow nature. He is not only to regulate nature; he is also supposed to step in actively and master nature. So there are only two moral principles to be maintained steadfastly: (1) every act between married people should be an act of love; (2) that calls for frequent abstention and the most urgent need.

Paul Chauchard and the partisans of the temperature method insist upon the benefits of some abstinence and some self-control. That may well be true, but should this abstinence be determined by the rhythm of physiological functions? Why should this question of self-mastery not be determined by the demands of love itself?

In short, should conjugal relations depend on physiological conditions or on moral dispositions?

Well, that is where the question stands; and it is in the Pope's lap. His special commissions are composed of representatives from all three viewpoints. There are those who will not budge from the traditional position, those who would allow the use of the pill to regulate nature, and those who say that once we go that far, we should go all the way.

The modern viewpoints seem to pose very solid objections against the arguments from nature. They say that temporal means of birth control are the same as spatial means. If you regulate intercourse by the calendar, you are doing the same thing as those who use other means. Moreover, respect for nature is not the moral rule for man. The artificial comes natural to man; his task is to improve and transform nature. In no other realm of his activity does this principle of respect for nature hold sway.

This whole question of respect for nature was once a burning issue with regard to mutilation and transplants. Theologians held that no one had the right to mutilate himself in order to give an organ to someone else. Man had to respect nature, and he did not have the final say over his own body.

Now the pressure of circumstances has forced theologians to re-evaluate their position. They now see that human dignity—justice and charity—justifies these operations which may seem contrary to nature. If we apply this principle to the question of sexual relations, it seems we can say that man has the right to employ "unnatural" means to limit his procreative powers.

Others also point out that it hardly seems very natural to say that a woman can have intercourse only during the period when she is least disposed towards it in terms of nature. Against this argument some object that there is no specially propitious or unpropitious period for the majority of women. But should majority rule here? If a few women find sexual satisfaction only in their fertile period, is it natural to deprive them of this satisfaction for a whole lifetime on the pretext that we must follow nature?

You should read what the theologians are saying on this question. And, by all means, read what lay people are writing on this topic because they have written some remarkable things.

So where do we stand at the moment? Well, many people hope that the Pope will not say anything. The question is not yet ripe, theologically speaking, because the schools of thought are still divided; and progress in Church doctrine must follow theological progress. This is not an area where inspiration operates; the question requires thought and reflection. It would be dangerous to adopt a position prematurely when the question has not yet been developed in all its dimensions.

Still others feel that the Pope is going to push back the limits imposed by Pius XII, but that he would like to do this without seeming to contradict the teaching of his predecessor.

At any rate, the principles seem evident enough: a procreative function grounded on reason and generosity, and conjugal relations that are truly acts of love. For the rest, it is up to the individual and his own conscience to apply these principles to his own case.

Now you may say to me: there are some contraceptive methods that are not natural, not felicitous, not ennobling. Undoubtedly that is true, but there are two points to be emphasized. (1) It is for married people, psychologists, and doctors to determine what is effective and harmonious in this area. The Church should not make pronouncements in this area. (2) This doctrine and this realm of human experience are in a state of ever continuing revision, because new techniques are invented every year. The Church need not panic about staying up with all these techniques. What she must do is proclaim the unchanging moral law; and it is not a law of techniques but a law of love.